WHAT ARE WE TO DO?

WHAT ARE
WE TO DO?

LIVING THE SERMON ON THE MOUNT

DAVID YOUNT

SHEED & WARD

Franklin, Wisconsin
Chicago

As an apostolate of the Priests of the Sacred Heart, a Catholic religious congregation, the mission of Sheed & Ward is to publish books of contemporary impact and enduring merit in Catholic Christian thought and action. The books published, however, reflect the opinion of their authors and are not meant to represent the official position of the Priests of the Sacred Heart.

2002

Sheed & Ward
7373 South Lovers Lane Road
Franklin, Wisconsin 53132
1-800-266-5564

Printed in the United States of America

Cover design: Kathy Kikkert Design
Interior design: GrafixStudio, Inc.
Jacket photograph by Erik Rank/Photonica

Scripture quotations are from J. B. Phillips, The New Testament in Modern English (Macmillan, 1972) © J. B. Phillips, 1972.

Old Testament selections are from the Holy Bible New International Version © International Bible Society, 1994.

Library of Congress Cataloging-in-Publication Data
Yount, David.
    What are we to do?: living the Sermon on the mount / David Yount.
    p.cm.
    ISBN 1-58051-118-X
    1. Sermon on the mount. 2. Christian life--Catholic authors.
    I. Title
    BT380.3.Y68-2002
    241.5′3--dc21   2001057714

1 2 3 4 5 / 05 04 03 02

DEDICATION

To the memory of
Donald Coggan,
101st Archbishop of Canterbury,
and for
John Crossin, OSFS,
Washington Theological Consortium

Ecce sacerdos magnus,
qui in diebus illis
placuit Deo.

ALSO BY DAVID YOUNT

Growing in Faith:
A Guide for the Reluctant Christian

Breaking through God's Silence:
A Guide to Effective Prayer

Spiritual Simplicity:
Simplify Your Life and Refresh Your Soul

Ten Thoughts to Take into Eternity:
Living in the Light of the Afterlife

Be Strong and Courageous:
Letters to My Children About Being Christian

TABLE OF
CONTENTS

PREFACE: What Are We to Do? ix

PART I: THE CALL 1

CHAPTER 1:   "Happy Are . . ." 3
               The Beatitudes
               (*Matthew 5:1–12*)

CHAPTER 2:   "You Are . . ." 21
               Salt and Light
               (*Matthew 5:13–6:4*)

CHAPTER 3:   "And Whenever You Pray . . ." 37
               Concerning Prayer
               (*Matthew 6:5–15*)

CHAPTER 4:   "And Whenever You Fast . . ." 53
               Concerning Fasting
               (*Matthew 6:16–34*)

CHAPTER 5:   "Do Not Judge . . ." 69
               Judging Others
               (*Matthew 7:1–29*)

PART II: THE COMMITMENT 85

CHAPTER 6:   The Will and the Way 87

CHAPTER 7:   Four Who Followed 103

CHAPTER 8:   The Mind of the Disciple 121

NOTES AND ACKNOWLEDGMENTS 135

The Christian ideal has not been tried
and found wanting.
It has been found difficult and left untried.
G. K. Chesterton

Humanly speaking it is impossible,
but with God anything is possible!
Matthew 19:26

PREFACE
WHAT ARE WE
TO DO?

In the heated 2000 race for the White House, reporters asked Vice President Gore how he would approach decision making as president of the United States. He replied that he would ask himself "What would Jesus do?"

Not to be outdone, George W. Bush proclaimed that he embraced Jesus of Nazareth as his personal model "because he changed my heart." Senator Joseph Lieberman, an Orthodox Jew running for vice president, asked the electorate to trust his political judgment because of his strict religious observance.

For the most part, the nation dismissed these personal pieties as political rhetoric. In a nation where ninety-five percent of the population believes in God, three-fourths pray each day, two-thirds belong to church, synagogue, or mosque, and more worship every Sabbath than watch the Super Bowl on but one Sunday of the year, invoking God is practical politics.

But can anyone presume to run a nation by asking what Jesus would do as president? After all, Jesus insisted that his kingdom was not of this world. Indeed, he was so impolitic that he threatened the political establishment of his time and was executed as a common criminal. His best "political" advice to his followers was to "give to Caesar what belongs to Caesar and to God what belongs to God" (Matthew 22:21).

Thus, it is ludicrous to imagine Jesus presiding over a multibillion dollar military establishment as commander-in-chief, when he clearly preached that "all those who take the sword will die by the sword" (Matthew 26:52). Echoing Jesus' teaching, the great reformer Martin Luther cautioned that it is impossible

> . . . to rule a country, let alone the entire world, by the gospel. God has placed human civil life under the dominion of natural reason, which has the ability to rule physical things. We need not look to scripture for advice.

In the wake of the September 11, 2001, attacks on New York and Washington, the president did not pause to invoke the gospel when he declared war on terrorism and called the nation to arms; nor did he ask what Jesus would do. As David Von Drehle noted in the Washington Post:

> The chief concern of a president should not be the condition of his immortal soul. His job is clearly stated in his oath: "to faithfully execute the office of the President" and to "preserve, protect, and defend the Constitution." These are secular responsibilities, and very serious ones. . . . The best a leader can expect, when going to war, is to be on the better side, morally and spiritually, of what will always be a bad business.

Nations may or may not have destinies, but only humans have souls. Jesus came not to save the world, but to redeem people.

Even in private life, the Christian who asks "What would Jesus do?" must remember that Jesus accomplished much that is beyond human capacities. Clearly, you and I cannot solve problems by working miracles. Conversely, we confront situations in contemporary life that Jesus did not: he did not marry, raise a family, work for a living, pay on a mortgage, or live long enough to suffer ill health and the problems of aging. In fact, it can be argued that Jesus took no time for a personal life at all, because his entire purpose was to live for others.

Given these cautions, we realize that the question is not "What would Jesus do?" but "What are *we* to do? Notice that the question is not "What am *I* to do?" but "What are *we* to do?" Jesus' message is universal. There are no distinctions among those who would answer his call and follow him. You and I are equally responsible to him and to one another. We cannot in conscience await a personal message but must answer his call together. It is not his duty to respond to us, but ours to answer him. In practice, of course, the question may yield only uncertain answers. It is, nonetheless, the single most pressing question if we are to abide by and embrace the gospel.

So, what are we to do? Very simply, we follow in Jesus' footsteps; we do precisely what the original disciples did. We hear Jesus' call to "follow me!" (Luke 9:59), knowing it is not an invitation but a command—a command, ultimately, to love and serve. And we respond without qualification.

In the first few centuries, pagans said of their Christian neighbors, "See how they love one another." Today, love remains the fundamental response to the question "What are we to do?" But how do we love in today's world? How do we make choices that are grounded in honest and authentic caring? For practical answers, we look to what Jesus did in his lifetime and to what he said—specifically his Sermon on the Mount (Matthew 5–7), at once the loftiest and most demanding revelation of what God had in mind when he created us.

As a boy, my parents encouraged me to be *good*, meaning "be obedient, be courteous, be fair, be truthful, be reliable." But I was not notably generous or loving. Still, my moral minimalism was enough to keep me out of trouble and to earn me the friendship of my peers and the confidence of the adults I sought to impress. When, as an adult, I encountered men and women whose goodness consisted of more than cautious virtue, I was humbled. As a college student, I once played host to the late Dorothy Day, who devoted her life to society's outcasts, doing what she had to do to follow Christ. People like Dorothy Day are not complacent. Rather, they love and they act on that love; they truly and unself-consciously follow the example of Christ, of whom St. Paul said "He went about doing good" (Acts 10:38).

Not *being* good, mind you, but *doing* good. Jesus did not rest on passive virtue. His goodness was active; he went out of his way to love others. In fact, he dismissed those who sought to flatter him, saying, "Why do you call me good? No one is good—only the one God" (Luke 18:19). He then challenged friends and enemies alike to "be perfect, like your heavenly Father" (Matthew 5:48).

If we approach life—its serious challenges and its day-to-day demands—asking the question "What are we to do given what Jesus did?" we will often be taxed with onerous answers that demand much of us; that is the nature of love. On those occasions, we will be close to Jesus, who, on the night before he died, asked of his Father, "If it is possible, let this cup pass from me," but added, "It must not be what I want, but what you want" (Matthew 26:39).

There are times—most of the time—when we act through habit, preference, or necessity, not virtue. So did Jesus. When he was tired, he slept. When he was hungry, he ate. When he was sorrowful, he wept. When he was cold, he sought shelter and warmth. Choosing what to wear or what to eat or when to rest is not a moral dilemma; rather, these actions are matters of taste and habit. But when it comes to the often overwhelming complexities of today's decision making, we cannot limit our actions to what is familiar, comfortable, or even preferred. Jesus faced serious consequences for what he said and did out of love; we do too.

Today's world is two millennia distant from that of the early Christians. We are required to make difficult decisions that Jesus' followers and the communities of the early church never faced. Because modern technology has turned our world into a global community, because today's weapons of war place our planet at risk of annihilation, because medical advances leave us facing dilemmas regarding life and death, we are burdened as never before with the question, "What are we to do?" Certainly we approach our choices with prayerful discernment, but Jesus' life offers little practical direction for the complex moral and ethical situations you and I face today. We can pray for guidance, but we cannot expect Jesus to assume the role of advice columnist. What we can look to Jesus for, however, is the model of how we must live and what decisions we must make, often in the face of adversity and life's challenges.

In most moral dilemmas, the choice is between doing something or doing nothing, risking something or risking nothing. As we ponder, again and again, his example, we notice that Jesus was a doer and a risker. He repeatedly stepped outside of cultural and political expectations to do that which put him at risk. What Jesus *would* do is what he *did*: he went about loving others and doing good.

For us, the best answers to "What are we to do?" are found in Jesus' Sermon on the Mount. Unfortunately, many Christians shy from the Sermon because the love preached there is so demanding. After all, if we elect to follow in Jesus' footsteps—to love as he loved—we will assuredly, like Jesus, find ourselves at risk. There is, however, this reassurance directly from his Sermon on the Mount: "Everyone then who hears these words of mine *and acts on them* will be like a wise man who built his house on rock. The rain fell, the floods came, and the winds blew and beat on that house, but it did not fall, because it had been founded on rock" (Matthew 7:24; emphasis added).

Nearly a century ago, when the *Times* of London asked prominent people of the time to submit responses to the question, "What's wrong with the world?" G. K. Chesterton offered the briefest answer. "What's wrong with the world? *Me!*" he replied. He noted famously that Christianity has not been tried and found wanting. Rather, it has been found to be difficult and has yet to be tried. In his Sermon on the Mount, Jesus demands that we try.

Let us join the multitudes who surrounded Jesus long ago and listen again to what it means to be a Christian. Let us follow him, acknowledging that we will falter, just as his first disciples did. But let us persevere in love, confident that God will forgive our clumsiness.

At the end of each chapter, I will suggest questions you may wish to ponder as you seek to follow in Jesus' footsteps, and I end each chapter with what, for me at least, is the big question Jesus raises for us with his invitation, "Follow me!

PART ONE

THE
CALL

ONE
"HAPPY ARE..."

THE BEATITUDES
(MATTHEW 5:1–12)

"How happy are those who know their need for God, for the kingdom of Heaven is theirs!

"How happy are those who know what sorrow means, for they will be given courage and comfort!

"Happy are those who claim nothing, for the whole earth will belong to them!

"Happy are those who are hungry and thirsty for true goodness, for they will be fully satisfied!

"Happy are the merciful, for they will have mercy shown to them!

"Happy are the utterly sincere, for they will see God!

"Happy are those who make peace, for they will be known as the sons of God!

"Happy are those who have suffered persecution for the cause of goodness, for the kingdom of Heaven is theirs!

"And what happiness will be yours when people blame you and ill-treat you and say all kinds of slanderous things against you for my sake!"
(Matthew 5:3–11)

Jesus launched his Sermon on the Mount with these aston-
ishing affirmations, turning conventional morality on its
head. Because the Beatitudes are so familiar to us, I have
used the less-familiar 1972 revised translation by J. B.
Phillips to underscore the shock value Jesus originally
intended. What Phillips lacks in poetic expression, he
delivers in clarity, which can only assist anyone who
approaches life asking "What are we to do?"

More traditional translations begin with *"Blessed* are . . . "
But Phillips's translation from the Greek is equally authoritative. Jesus promises that whoever takes on these qualities
of life will be *happy*—beatifically so! To be blessed is to be
happy, because our lives coincide with God's intention—the
creatures he means us to be, bearing his own image.

Whoever follows Christ is in a happy state of heart and
mind, although it would be a stretch to claim that the disciple necessarily *feels* happy. Still, with hearts and minds in
alignment with God's intention, we can bear the burden of
persecution with equanimity, even joy. The true disciple is
in a love affair with God and is literally carefree.

Philip Yancey notes that "any Greek scholar will tell you
the word 'blessed' is far too sedate and beatific to carry the
percussive force Jesus intended. The Greek word conveys
something like a short cry of joy, 'Oh, you lucky person!'"

THE SENSE OF THE SERMON

The sermon comprises chapters 5, 6, and 7 of Matthew's
Gospel. There is a shorter version in Luke set on a plain.
Whether Jesus actually said all these things at any one time
is idle speculation. Taken together, however, these are his
directions for how we are to choose and how we are to act
and how we are to be motivated. They form the basis for
answering the question, "What are we to do?" As Hans
Küng says in his seminal work, *On Being a Christian*, the
Sermon on the Mount "aims at taking God's will absolutely
seriously."

As a child I was taught that the Sermon on the Mount
consisted of "counsels of perfection" designed for saints—
mere optional behavior for us "non-saints." But in view of

Jesus' command that we follow him, he means his words to be taken seriously.

Also clear is Jesus' audience—to whom he was speaking then and now. The sermon is addressed not to the righteous, but to those who seek seriously to imitate Christ and possess the humility to seek forgiveness when they fail. The very setting of the sermon, in fact, is critical to its understanding. It begins: "When Jesus saw the vast crowds, he went up the hill-side and, after he had sat down his disciples came to him. Then he began his teaching by saying to them . . . "

To whom does the word *them* refer? To the vast crowds? No, at least not immediately. Although the multitudes constitute the audience, Jesus is speaking to them *about* his disciples. They are the ones who have left everything to follow him, and he uses the Beatitudes precisely to describe them. Jesus' followers are poor, for all they have is him. They are sorrowful, humble, merciful, sincere, persecuted, and blamed. And they are peacemakers. What else could they be under the circumstances? Imperfect as they are, they have chosen to cast their lot with Jesus, transforming them into the salt of the earth, light of the world, and heirs to God's kingdom. They are not just "blessed." They are "happy" in their new state.

While the sermon refers to the disciples, however, it addresses the multitudes and the ages, including us. It also reflects the fact that Jesus' disciples—then and now—already exemplify the new values of the kingdom.

THE "HARD SAYINGS" OF THE BEATITUDES

In the Beatitudes that begin the sermon, Jesus is "telling it like it is," making clear *how things are* for those who follow him: they are blessed and happy in imitating him. But he adds how a disciple must act, and here we confront what have been called Jesus' "hard sayings":

- We must not be angry with one another.

- We must forgive one another before we seek God's pardon.

- We must not only refrain from adultery, but from lust.

- We must not divorce for any reason other than unfaithfulness.

- We must tell the truth without conditions.

- We must turn the other cheek to our persecutors, and give to those who would borrow from us.

- We must love our enemies and refrain from criticizing others.

As if this weren't an onerous-enough agenda, Jesus adds that "if your right eye leads you astray, pluck it out and throw it away," and "if your right hand leads you astray, cut it off and throw it away; it is better for you to lose one of your members than that your whole body should go to the rubbish-heap" (Matthew 5:29–30).

What are we to make of this? Is it another example of hyperbole that Jesus often used to underscore the moral of what he is saying? Of course: Jesus doesn't prescribe self-mutilation. Still, he wouldn't use such drastic figures of speech unless what he is saying is meant to be taken seriously. These are permanent values of the kingdom.

THE REWARDS, THEN AND NOW

Those who imitate Christ are lucky because he assigns them rewards in his kingdom. In his own words, "The kingdom is theirs." They will be given courage and comfort, and the whole earth will belong to them. They will be fully satisfied and will have mercy shown to them. They will see God, and they will be known as the children of God. Their reward in heaven is magnificent.

Rest assured this is not a pie-in-the-sky promise, but an immediate one, because Jesus has *already* inaugurated God's kingdom. There is no waiting to see God, because the disciples have seen Jesus. The kingdom is theirs now. They are already children of God. The whole earth belongs to them now because Jesus has claimed and redeemed it. God has already awarded his followers courage, comfort, and mercy.

But at what price? What did—and does—this happy and blessed kingdom cost the disciples of Jesus? Humility, repentance, simplicity, goodness, mercy, sincerity, reconciliation—and persecution. Why persecution? Because Jesus' disciples have rejected the world's values of wealth, pride, power, vanity, and luxury, and the world will mock them for it. Jesus acknowledged that he was a "sign of contradiction"—not just misunderstood by people, but actually hated by those he embarrassed. Those who seek to imitate him are not masochists, welcoming ill-treatment. Rather, they are realists who acknowledge that Jesus himself was persecuted.

In the master's company, Jesus' disciples cannot help but be humble-minded. Cognizant of their sins and shortcomings, they are remorseful. The spartan life they lead, indeed, is poor in many ways. Imitating Jesus, they have become merciful, justice-seeking peacemakers. Evasion is no longer an alternative, so they must be sincere. They are scorned, just as Jesus is.

But an understanding of their rewards did not come easily. The apostle Peter, in fact, challenged Jesus: We have given up everything to follow you; what will be our reward? Peter's insistence is so true to human nature that it serves to make the gospel account credible. It is exactly what I would have demanded had Jesus told me to follow him: What's in it for me?

Critics of Christianity complain that, since every human being expects a reward for effort, the only difference between them and us is that they pursue their rewards this side of eternity, whereas Christians are content to wait. When Peter confronted Jesus, he was not content to wait for his reward. Over time, however, he and his fellow disciples discovered that the life Jesus prescribed for his followers contains its own rewards. As their love for him grew it was reciprocated. At length it dawned on them that the life Jesus prescribed is what the Creator intended for everyone from the outset. The Beatitudes exemplify life in God's kingdom, where rewards are not merited but rather are signs of God's generosity.

J. B. Phillips's translation of the Beatitudes presents eight in total. A closer look at each one will clarify what

Jesus means and what he calls his disciples to live. With that better understanding, we—Jesus' disciples today—will be better prepared to answer the question "What are we to do?"

THOSE WHO KNOW THEIR NEED FOR GOD (MATTHEW 5:3)

Most translations of the first Beatitude have Jesus proclaiming "Blessed are the poor." In Luke's parallel account, Jesus is clearer: "Blessed are the poor *in spirit.*" Doubtless, most of those who heard Jesus were materially poor. But Jesus was not pandering to the destitute or praising want in his sermon. J. B. Phillips prefers the expression "those who know their need for God." In any case, Jesus' valuation of "poverty" contrasts sharply with what he said about the rich:

> "Believe me, a rich man will find it very difficult to enter the kingdom of Heaven. Yes, I repeat, a camel could more easily squeeze through the eye of a needle than a rich man get into the kingdom of God!" (Matthew 19:23–24)

Jesus' moral is that wealth of any sort is a distraction from the kingdom rather than the key to open it. Be it the wealth of material goods, security, prestige, pleasure, or power, wealth is a blinding force that veils the kingdom's treasures. Happily, the poor are not distracted: all they have is Jesus. He is their wealth. The poor in spirit empty their lives to make room for him. Clearly, Jesus' closest followers misunderstood his meaning. They "were simply amazed to hear this, and said, 'then who can possible be saved?'" To which Jesus replied, "Humanly speaking it is impossible; but with God anything is possible" (Matthew 19:25–26).

The poor in spirit are happy; the impoverished, however, are miserable. Just as Jesus hates the sin but loves the sinner, he hates poverty but loves the poor—and that is his call to those who wish to be his disciples. In one of his most demanding parables, Jesus addressed what his disciples should do. "I was hungry and you gave me nothing to eat."

When they in turn asked, "Lord, when did we ever see you hungry?" he answered "I assure you that whatever you failed to do to the humblest of my brothers, you failed to do to me" (Matthew 25:42, 44–45).

The statistics regarding poverty around the world are staggering. Today some 790 million men, women, and children in poor countries around the world are malnourished. Two of every five children in the Third World are permanently stunted in growth, one in three is underweight, and one in ten is unlikely to survive to adulthood. Another thirty-four million go to bed hungry every night in the world's *richest* nations.

Poverty in the United States is a scandal. More than one of every eight Americans is poor. One in five youngsters lives below the poverty line, undernourished, poorly educated, and deprived of adequate health care. Thirty million Americans do not know where their next meal is coming from. Millions are homeless. Since 1970, despite general prosperity, the percentage of American children living in poverty increased by one-third.

Yet, even as the poor go hungry, three of every five Americans are overweight; one third of that number are obese. Our national fixation with weight loss feeds a diet industry that absorbs $34 billion every year.

The plight of the poor, however, is a hunger that goes far deeper than the pain of an empty stomach. The humiliation, powerlessness, and isolation of being "a poor person" gradually erode the human spirit, leaving it, like the body, on the brink of starvation. I saw this kind of starvation of spirit when I was a theological student in Paris in the 1960s. I joined young French Christians to beg for leftover meat and vegetables from markets and restaurants, then helped make a stew to feed the homeless and destitute. Every evening at dusk a line of poor men and women formed in a twelfth-century church courtyard close to Notre Dame Cathedral, where we distributed food until it was gone. Few of our guests expressed gratitude; many were surly. Some even fought among themselves for larger portions.

This experience with "the poor" was eye-opening. The poor were ungrateful. Then again, why should they be grateful for a mere bowl of stew and a piece of bread?

Didn't they deserve more, not because of their virtue but because they were God's own sons and daughters, as we are—as those of us serving them? We are tempted to leave the needs of the poor to government. That is not what Jesus did. His words still resonate with anyone who would imitate him: "I assure you that whatever you failed to do to the humblest of my brothers, you failed to do to me."

Clearly, Jesus was countercultural—and called his disciples to be the same. He lived and preached, as is so evident in his Sermon on the Mount—that what the world values is of little use in the kingdom.

The poor crippled hero of George Gershwin's opera *Porgy and Bess* lived in the peace of that kingdom. He admitted that he had "plenty of nuthin'," and then counted his blessings. "No use complaining: I got my Lord," he sang, and "heaven the whole day long." He didn't fret or worry "'long as I'm well," never strived, but was "glad I'm alive."

Author Monika Hellwig agrees that those who have little appreciate the good news of the gospel more than the affluent. They realize they need redemption, and knowing that, they depend on God and one another. They find security not in things but in people. They are not self-important. They grasp the difference between life's necessities and its luxuries. They have learned to be patient and, as a result, they suffer less anxiety because they know they can survive hardship. For them the gospel is a gift, not a burden. With less to lose than the rest of us, they welcome God's love with gratitude.

In his book, *Good News*, J. B. Phillips contrasts the values that characterize life in the kingdom of heaven with the values of the secular world:

> Happy are the "pushers": for they get on in the world.
> Happy are the hard-boiled: for they never let life hurt them.
> Happy are those who complain: for they get their own way in the end.
> Happy are the blasé: for they never worry over their sins.
> Happy are the slave-drivers: for they get results.

Happy are the knowledgeable men of the world: for
they know their way around.
Happy are the trouble-makers: for they make people
take notice of them.

Of course, only poverty that is freely chosen is virtuous.
Material poverty is a scandal, but poverty of *spirit* can be
obtained by simplifying one's life, by laying down the bur-
dens of unneeded possessions and ambitions and the anxieties that accompany them. Philip Yancey in his book *The
Jesus I Never Knew*, acknowledges that the poor are no more
virtuous than the rest of us, but they are less likely to *pretend* to be virtuous.

THOSE WHO KNOW WHAT SORROW MEANS (MATTHEW 5:4)

The traditional translation of the second Beatitude is
"Blessed are those who mourn," which the English apolo-
gist John R. W. Stott suggests implies the paradoxical message, "Happy are the unhappy." That clearly was not Jesus'
intention. The context of the Sermon on the Mount is Jesus'
call for repentance, his affirmation of those who feel *remorse*
for the harm they have caused others. Certainly Jesus' love
and grace are with those who mourn and grieve, but the
second Beatitude calls for contrition.

I recall incidents during the years I worked in public
relations in Washington, D.C. The advice we gave to officials caught in compromising situations was to admit their
wrongdoing and say they were sorry. Too often it stopped
there, and their "sorrow" represented nothing more than
their embarrassment at being caught. As Stott says, "Confession is one thing, contrition is another." Today, people
with outrageous lifestyles compete to appear on television
talk shows to proudly reveal their crimes and misde-
meanors to perfect strangers.

Remorse is something else. In the 1662 *Book of Common
Prayer* Archbishop Cranmer included a prayer of public
confession which contains these words: "We acknowledge
and bewail our manifold sins and wickedness." The word-
ing may sound quaint, but the sentiment is real. Saint Paul

groaned, "Wretched man that I am! Who will deliver me from this body of death?" (Romans 7:24)

Those who seek to imitate Christ must first be honest with themselves. The Catholic, for example, who has ready access to the sacrament of penance may fall into a confessional routine but fail to feel remorse. Or the evangelical Christian whose experience of being born again leaves him with a sense of plentiful amazing grace may altogether forget that he is still a sinner. Both lack self-honesty. Martin Luther described the sinner's situation crudely, comparing God's grace to snow covering a human dung heap. Other commentators claim that grace utterly transforms us, but experience suggests that the reformed sinner is still a sinner. Yet Jesus pronounces such a person happy and promises to encourage and comfort him. As Stott reminds us:

> Jesus wept over the sins of others, over their bitter consequences in judgment and death, and over the impenitent city which would not receive him. We too should weep more over the evil in the world . . .

That is what we are to do.

THOSE WHO CLAIM NOTHING (MATTHEW 5:5)

We tend to think of the third Beatitude, in its reference to the meek, as being addressed to the timid losers, the wimps, the Walter Mittys of the world, those who shrink from life's challenges and rewards. Since Jesus referred to himself as meek, the word clearly has lost the power it possessed in his sermon. In the gospels he was never the "gentle Jesus, meek and mild" to whom we were introduced as young children.

J. B. Phillips's translation avoids the word *meek* altogether, substituting the phrase "those who claim nothing." The Greek adjective means "gentle, humble, courteous, considerate." When the elder George Bush called for a "kinder, gentler America" in his inaugural address on January 20, 1989, he was roundly criticized by the pundits for promoting feminine virtues. But kindness and gentleness are sensible attitudes for Christians who possess a true estimate of themselves and possess the courage not to pretend to be more than they are.

Celebrities often admit that they are shy and self-doubting. Some even acknowledge that they have a low opinion of themselves. But when they perform, they assume a different persona, like a mask, and pretend they are that artificial character. Happy, Jesus says, are those who claim to be no more than they are—sinners in need of repentance. As Martyn Lloyd-Jones notes in his *Studies on the Sermon on the Mount*:

> Meekness is essentially a true view of oneself, expressing itself in attitude and conduct with respect to others . . . The man who is truly meek is the one who is truly amazed that God and man can think of him as well as they do and treat him as well as they do.

During the years when I was president of the National Press Foundation I routinely attended black-tie dinners with the Washington press corps at which the president of the United States was the "honored" guest. The current occupant of the White House was typically introduced by a comedian, who poked fun at the president for his recent personal and professional foibles. Not only was the president expected to laugh at jokes delivered at his expense, but he was required to respond with a self-deprecating speech. "Roasted" by others, he was expected to finish the job himself.

That is what Jesus had in mind: being meek and honest about ourselves and taking criticism that cuts to the bone (and not always the funny bone).

That is what we are to do.

THOSE WHO HUNGER AND THIRST FOR TRUE GOODNESS (MATTHEW 5:6)

The usual translation of the fourth Beatitude favors the word "righteousness" rather than "true goodness," obscuring Jesus' demand for both integrity and the pursuit of social justice. The disciple must be good within and without.

Those who would imitate Christ cannot be satisfied with their own righteousness as their ticket to salvation. Rather, they must hunger and thirst for God's justice for others. Although we will find perfect fairness only in God's kingdom, it can be approximated this side of eternity in the practice of genuine compassion.

In his commentary on the sermon, Luther explained the requirements of this Beatitude bluntly:

> The command to you is not to crawl into a corner or into the desert, but to run out . . . and offer your hands and your feet and your whole body, and wager everything you have and can do. (You must have) a hunger and thirst for righteousness that can never be curbed or stopped or sated, one that looks for nothing except the accomplishment and maintenance of justice, despising everything that hinders this goal. If you cannot make the world completely pious, then do what you can.

Whoever would imitate Christ cannot be content to stop with remorse, the essence of the third Beatitude. Rather, Jesus' disciples must actively seek the future that God intends for everyone, a future grounded in a present that seeks integrity in the world, that liberates humankind from oppression, and that promotes justice in the courts, in gender and race relations, in commerce, and in the family. Seeking first the kingdom of God is not a quest for one's own satisfaction, but for all God's creatures. Unlike the officials in the gospel who ignored the wounded man on the road, Christians must be Good Samaritans, driven by compassion and the prospect of justice for all.

Today, our world is hardly devoid of parables that manifest such true goodness. If you reflect on the events surrounding the tragic death of Princess Diana in Paris, for example, you will recall that French law *requires* that anyone at the scene of an accident be a Good Samaritan or otherwise be liable for prosecution. In brief, that nation made it a crime to evade responsibility for others in need. Also, the same responsibility to seek justice was underscored in the final episode of the television series *Seinfeld*, when the shallow principals were jailed for a whole series of irresponsible incidents in their lives. Finally, in the General Confession in *The Book of Common Prayer*, Christians ask God's forgiveness not only for what they have done, but for what they have failed to do.

This is what we are to do.

THOSE WHO ARE MERCIFUL (MATTHEW 5:7)

The fifth Beatitude addresses mercy and justice. Justice is typically expressed in law. People go to court to seek it, and they fight with one another to get their due. In practice, the pursuit of justice is antagonistic. Too often it is motivated by revenge. The courts produce winners and losers—not equal justice for all. Those who hunger and thirst for God's justice recognize that many of their fellow men and women fall through the cracks in the justice system. These people know the need for mercy. As Dietrich Bonhoeffer notes in *The Cost of Discipleship*, these people

> . . . take upon themselves the distress and humiliation and sin of others. They have an irresistible love for the down-trodden, the sick, the wretched, the wronged, the outcast and all who are tortured with anxiety. They go out and seek all who are enmeshed in the toils of sin and guilt. No distress is too great . . .

Justice seeks equal treatment for all. Mercy recognizes that justice this side of eternity is imperfect. Most of the peoples in the world are in need, but those in the developed world are more affluent. The fortunate must show mercy to the less fortunate.

I often receive mail from men in prison who read my syndicated newspaper column. Some express remorse for their crimes; most merely feel self-pity for their plight. But all are lonely and appreciate a friendly letter and a reminder that God is swift to forgive, even when people are not. Jesus once challenged his disciples, saying, "I was in prison, and you did not visit me." When was that? they demanded, and he answered, "What you do to the least of my brothers, you do to me" (Matthew 25:36, 45).

This is what we are to do.

THOSE WHO ARE UTTERLY SINCERE (MATTHEW 5:8)

The traditional translation of the sixth Beatitude refers to "the pure in heart." G. K. Chesterton once told a story about the human heart, imagining an alien's first sight of a human being. The visitor from outer space, Chesterton suggested, would note that the left and right sides of men and women are mirror images of each other. Ears, arms, hands, legs, and feet match each other. Nose, mouth, neck, and torso are the same left and right. We are symmetrical.

Being of a scientific bent of mind, Chesterton's alien would assume that the human heart—the organ of affection—is in the middle of the body and perfectly proportioned. However, he would be wrong. The human heart is off center and imperfectly formed.

Jesus demands that we have our heart in the right place. That requires a change of heart, a remaking of our affections, turning away from self-service and toward God. It means making love the rule of our lives.

This is what we are to do.

THOSE WHO MAKE PEACE (MATTHEW 5:9)

The seventh Beatitude emphasizes the importance of not only *being* at peace or *being* a peaceful people, but *actively making* peace. Just as Jesus came to reconcile humankind with their Creator, they must reconcile with one another. Peace cannot be assumed, because it is not simply the absence of conflict. Rather, peace is the creation of accord. Nor is peace an armed truce, a mere agreement to disagree. True peace is based on justice and the forgiveness and love of enemies, who do not thereby necessarily become our friends, but our brothers and sisters nevertheless.

Later in the gospel Jesus would seem to contradict himself:

> "Never think that I have come to bring peace upon the earth. No, I have not come to bring peace but a sword! For I have come to set a man against his own

father, a daughter against her own mother, and a daughter-in-law against her mother-in-law. A man's enemies will be those who live in his own house" (Matthew 10:34–36).

But Jesus immediately explains himself:

"Anyone who puts his love for father or mother above his love for me does not deserve to be mine, and he who loves son or daughter more than me is not worthy of me, and neither is the man who refuses to take up his cross and follow my way. The man who has found his life will lose it, but the man who has lost it for my sake will find it" (Matthew 10:37–39).

Jesus himself is a sign of contradiction. He will cause conflict between those who prefer themselves before him. Taken together, his Beatitudes specify a life at variance with the values of the world. Accordingly, John Stott proclaims Christianity to be a "counter-culture." Christians are dissidents. This Beatitude follows from the last, that of "sincerity" or "purity of heart," because only the utterly sincere—those who harbor no grudges and seek no advantage—can effect reconciliation.

Still, the peace of God is not peace at any price for the sake of covering up real conflict; it is not appeasement. Rather, it is the courageous naming and risking involved in facing the real chaos of discord. German theologian Dietrich Bonhoeffer was executed in a concentration camp because his faith prompted him to defy the Nazis and seek to end the horrors they committed. When Bonhoeffer took the Nazis to task, they expressed no sorrow; instead, they killed him. Jesus took his critics to task as well, and they nailed him to a cross.

Peacemakers cannot forget an injury when it is neither admitted nor regretted. But they can forgive their enemies for the same reason Jesus forgave those who put him to death: "Father, forgive them; they do not know what they are doing" (Luke 23:34).

This is what we are to do.

THOSE WHO HAVE SUFFERED PERSECUTION (MATTHEW 5:11–12)

The eighth Beatitude proposes a disconcerting irony: those who seek peace and justice must expect to be opposed and persecuted. Jesus, however, was merely noting a fact of universal experience: people who try to set things right are themselves wronged. Still, Jesus' disciples are not masochists seeking to suffer. Rather, they are realists accepting persecution as the price of imitating Christ. Suffering is the sign of authentic Christianity. Jesus tells his disciples, "They persecuted the prophets before your time in the same way" (Matthew 5:12).

But how can persecution be cause for rejoicing? Jesus answers: "Because my disciples suffer on my account" (see Matthew 5:11)—out of loyalty to him and his standards. "With every Beatitude," Bonhoeffer noted before his execution, "the gulf is widened between the disciples and the people . . . Suffering, then, is the badge of true discipleship. The disciple is not above his master."

Preparing the Augsburg Confession, Luther defined the Church as the community of those "who are persecuted and martyred for the gospel's sake." Luther's own latter-day disciple, Martin Luther King, Jr., acknowledged that "Christianity has always insisted that the cross we bear precedes the crown we wear . . . To be a Christian one must take up his cross, with all its difficulties and agonizing and tension-packed content, and carry it until that very cross leaves its mark upon us and redeems us to that more excellent way which comes only with suffering."

Once again, we need not speculate about what Jesus *would* do, but acknowledge what he actually did. He suffered.

The final Beatitude expands on the treatment the disciple can expect:

> "And what happiness will be yours when people blame you and ill-treat you and say all kinds of slanderous things against you for my sake! Be glad

then, yes, be tremendously glad—for your reward
in Heaven is magnificent" (Matthew 5:11–12).

Jesus suffered the same abuse. His critics accused him
of blasphemy and acting unlawfully on the Sabbath. The
Pharisees accused him of allying himself with sinners and
casting out demons with Satan's power. The crowds jeered
him and mocked him, while others called him the devil, a
glutton, and a drunkard. At the end of his life, the abuse
became physical.

In the wake of the terrorist attacks on America, the
nation proclaimed its innocence and righteously retaliated
with force. Christians joined with their fellow citizens in con-
demning those who would abuse us, and supported a war.

Jesus' sermon does not address the acts of nations. But
we know that in his personal life he did not meet violence
with violence. Most Christians believe that they are
required to defend loved ones from physical harm, and
most agree that they are justified in defending themselves,
but not by violent means or in the spirit of revenge, but in
the interests of peace.

A Christian is not someone who merely admires or
believes in Christ, but one who does what he does.

This is what we are to do.

☞ ☞ ☞

Late in his life, anguished in conscience, the great Russ-
ian novelist Leo Tolstoy made a heroic attempt to follow
the Sermon on the Mount. He failed miserably, because he
believed Jesus meant for him to literally impoverish himself and his family, to toil with his hands, and to cease sex-
ual relations with his wife. He ended his life in near
suicidal exhaustion, blaming himself for his weakness, but
acknowledging that Jesus' standards were correct.

Tolstoy misunderstood the sermon by treating it as
law—attempting to adhere to its letter rather than its spirit.
But he was right in this: he humbly acknowledged his
frailty and accepted God's forgiveness.

That surely is what we are to do.

Questions to Ponder

1. How did Jesus turn conventional morality on its head?

2. How can Christians expect to be happy if they claim nothing and suffer persecution?

3. Are God's rewards proportional to the rigors Jesus proposes?

4. How did the first disciples, imperfect as they were, exemplify the Sermon on the Mount?

5. Why did Jesus favor the poor over the rich?

Following in Jesus' Steps

1. *Peacemaking.* What can I do to reconcile myself with my enemies?

2. *Poverty.* Americans spend more on dieting than on feeding the world's hungry majority. What is the Christian's responsibility for people in need?

3. *Remorse.* Can I admit my shortcomings and still be effective?

4. *Humor.* Can I make an honest assessment of myself and still retain a healthy sense of humor?

5. *Justice and mercy.* What can I do to ensure that my heart is sincere?

The Big Question

Jesus said, "I assure you that whatever you failed to do to the humblest of my brothers, you failed to do to me." What can I do to ensure that I do not fail him?

TWO

"YOU ARE . . ."

SALT AND LIGHT
(MATTHEW 5:13–6:4)

When Jesus concluded his litany of revolutionary teachings, he knew his disciples were confused, so he offered images of salt and light to demonstrate to his followers their role in the world.

To help us understand the challenge Jesus presented, then and now, a more contemporary analogy is helpful. Philip M. Harter of Stanford's School of Medicine has a unique way of looking at human diversity and need that can help us see the essential need for our mission as salt and light to a desperate world. Harter has determined that, were the world's current population compressed into a village of just 100 citizens, this is what our community would look like:

- 57 villagers would be Asian

- 21 would be European

- 14 would be from the western hemisphere

- 8 would be African

- 52 would be female; 48 male

- 70 would be non-white; 30 white

- 70 would be non-Christian; 30 Christian

- 89 would be heterosexual; 11 gay

Of more importance:

- 6 persons would possess 59% of the village's wealth—all of them Americans, whereas

- 80 would live in substandard housing

- 70 would be illiterate

- 50 would suffer from malnutrition

- 1 would have a college education and own a computer

- 1 would be dying

When you and I locate ourselves within this micro-community, we find ourselves to be members of a small advantaged minority. As Dr. Harter notes:

- If you woke this morning with more health than illness, you are more fortunate than the million who will survive this week.

- If you have never experienced the danger of battle, the loneliness of imprisonment, the agony of torture, or the pangs of starvation, you are ahead of half a billion people in the world.

- If you have food in the refrigerator, clothes on your back, a roof overhead, and a place to sleep, you are richer than three-fourths of the world's people.

- And because you can worship God publicly without fear of harassment, arrest, torture, or death, you are more fortunate than three billion people in the world.

The Disciple's Responsibility (Matthew 5:13–16)

Every one of our fellow men and women, without exception, is God's creature, bearing his image. Or, as Quakers prefer to say, there is "that of God" in each of us. All have the same heavenly Father. Jesus became human and died for the sole purpose of redeeming all of us. Thus, we all possess the same hope and destiny as citizens of God's kingdom.

But, as Dr. Harter's condensed global community clearly demonstrates, few know hope and love, and fewer still sense God's grace and care. Making his good news known is the responsibility of Jesus' disciples, those who hear and act on Jesus' words from the Sermon on the Mount. These are the ones Jesus calls light to the world and salt of the earth:

> "You are the earth's salt. But if the salt should become tasteless, what can make it salt again? It is completely useless and can only be thrown out of doors and stamped under foot. You are the world's light—it is impossible to hide a town built on the top of a hill. Men do not light a lamp and put it under a bucket. They put it on a lampstand and it gives light for everybody in the house. Let your light shine like that in the sight of men. Let them see the good things you do and praise your Father in Heaven" (Matthew 5:13–16).

In Jesus' time, before refrigeration, salt was necessary not only to flavor food but to preserve meat and fish. In a world lit only by fire, nights were long and dark. No one could find his way without a candle or torch. Salt and light are metaphors for the Christian's influence for good in the world. Those who imitate Christ preserve his promise and enlighten the world.

In the prologue to his Gospel, St. John calls Jesus the light of the world: "In him appeared life, and this life was the light of mankind. The light still shines in the darkness and the darkness has never put it out. . . . That was the true light which shines upon every man" (John 1:4–5, 9).

Those who seek to answer the question "What are we to do?" will preserve and enlighten the world, doing good. They will be salt of the earth and light to the world. If they lose their savor or hide their light, the world Jesus came to redeem will revert to darkness and decay.

For the disciples of Jesus there can be no compromise with a dark and decadent world. Martyn Lloyd-Jones argues: "The glory of the gospel is that when the Church is absolutely different from the world, she invariably attracts it. It is then that the world is made to listen to her message, though it may hate it at first."

TELLING THE TRUTH (MATTHEW 5:17–20)

Clearly, the world's people need food, shelter, medical care, literacy, security, and education. But they also need the truth, and they need the faith and hope that come with it. In our time, unfortunately, *proselytism* has become a dirty word, and religious faith is no longer a subject to be raised in polite society.

John Stott retorts: "As the disciples of Christ, we are not to conceal the truth we know or the truth of what we are. We are not to pretend to be other than what we are, but be willing for our Christianity to be visible to all." Dietrich Bonhoeffer adds: "A community of Jesus which seeks to hide itself has ceased to follow him."

Jesus told the truth without pressuring people or berating them. When he casually sat himself down on a hillside to encourage and affirm his disciples—to call them "happy" and "blessed"—the gathering multitudes began to hear his words as well. Without a promotional campaign or marketing program, Jesus brought only good news and condemned only religious pretense. By his example, he led people to the truth and made faith attractive because he did good. In similar fashion, we do not have to get on a soapbox to deliver the gospel; rather, we need only live our faith to be eloquent by example. Others will believe because they see what our faith has done for us.

The truth is that Jesus has already changed everything while destroying nothing:

> "You must not think that I have come to abolish the Law or the Prophets; I have not come to abolish them but to complete them. Indeed, I assure you that, while Heaven and earth last, the Law will not

lose a single dot or comma until its purpose is complete. That means that whoever now relaxes one of the least of these commandments and teaches men to do the same will himself be called least in the kingdom of Heaven. But whoever teaches and practices them will be called great in the kingdom of Heaven. For I tell you that your goodness must be a far better thing than the goodness of the scribes and Pharisees before you can set foot in the kingdom of Heaven at all!" (Matthew 5:17–20)

With the Beatitudes, Jesus established a new moral order while holding his disciples to the covenant conveyed by God through Moses. There are no excuses. Bonhoeffer remarks of Jesus: "He has in fact nothing to add to the commandments of God, except this, that he keeps them . . . It was an error of Israel to put the law in God's place, to make the law their God, and their God a law." The "better righteousness" of Christ is to love God, not to idolize his rules. It is to follow him. Jesus contrasts his disciples with the scribes and Pharisees, who consider their rulekeeping to be personal achievement. The disciples accept that their righteousness is a *gift*, and that it belongs, as Bonhoeffer notes, "only to the poor, the tempted, the hungry, the meek, the peacemakers, the persecuted—who endure their lot for the sake of Jesus."

The Better Righteousness (Matthew 5:21–26)

"You have heard that it was said to the people in the old days, 'Thou shalt not murder,' and anyone who does so must stand his trial. But I say to you that anyone who is angry with his brother must stand his trial; anyone who contemptuously calls his brother a fool must face the supreme court; and anyone who looks down on his brother as a lost soul is himself heading straight for the fire of destruction. So that if, while you are offering your gift at the altar, you should remember that your brother has something against you, you must leave your gift there before the altar and go away. Make

your peace with your brother first, then come and
offer your gift. Come to terms quickly with your
opponent at law while you are on the way to court.
Otherwise he may hand you over to the judge and
the judge in turn hand you over to the officer of the
court and you will be thrown into prison. Believe
me, you will never get out again till you have paid
your last farthing!"

For the first time in his sermon, Jesus refers to himself—
"But I say to you . . . "—affirming that he, as God's Son, not
only keeps the law perfectly, but is, in fact, its author. He
condemns murder because God alone gives life and has
power over life and death. But Jesus goes further, insisting
that everyone is our brother, and that anger itself is a kind
of murder, because hatred, contempt, slander, and cursing
are intended to destroy.

The proposition that "sticks and stones may break my
bones, but words will never hurt me" flies against all experience of reality. Physical wounds heal in time, but we all
know or have experienced firsthand how words can permanently break a heart, destroy trust, or ruin a reputation.

Jesus makes no exception here for *righteous* anger
among his disciples. Although later in his ministry there
are instances of Jesus' own anger—driving the money
changers from the temple, calling his enemies on their
hypocrisy—his disciples have no right to indulge their
master's power to judge another, because they are no better than their brother or sister.

Is this prohibition to anger impossible to keep? Not if
properly understood. In his sermon Jesus does not qualify
his condemnation of anger, but it is clear that he is not talking about irritability, exasperation, and bad temper, which
are inescapable emotions. Nor is he talking about the anger
that motivates us to speak out in the name of justice and
peace. It is only the anger that we nurture and use as a
weapon against others that Jesus condemns.

Paul understood the distinction: "If you are angry, be
sure that it is not a sinful anger. Never go to bed angry—
don't give the devil that sort of foothold" (Ephesians 4:26);
and "Put all these things behind you: evil temper, furious
rage, malice, insults, and shouted abuse" (Colossians 3:8).

To follow Jesus' example, the disciple is justified in hating the sin but loving the sinner.

MAN AND WOMAN (MATTHEW 5:27–32)

> "You have heard that it was said to the people in the old days, 'Thou shalt not commit adultery.' But I say to you that every man who looks at a woman lustfully has already committed adultery with her—in his heart. Yes, if your right eye leads you astray pluck it out and throw it away; it is better for you to lose one of your members than that your whole body should be thrown on to the rubbish heap. Yes, if your right hand leads you astray cut it off and throw it away; it is better for you to lose one of your members than that your whole body should go to the rubbish-heap. It also used to be said that whoever divorces his wife must give her a proper certificate of divorce. But I say to you that whoever divorces his wife except on the ground of unfaithfulness is making her an adulteress. And whoever marries the woman who has been divorced also commits adultery."

Here Jesus condemns the *cultivation* of lust—like the nurturing of anger—and for the same reason: it abuses another person and distracts the disciple from faithful love. Of course, one may *feel* desire without indulging its consummation. To find a man or woman sexually attractive is only appreciative and passive, not seductive and active.

Feminists understand the distinction perfectly. That's why they condemn pornography, which not only excites lust but treats women as objects rather than persons. "Jesus does not impose intolerable restrictions on his disciples," Bonhoeffer notes. "He does not forbid them to look at anything, but bids them look on him." To cultivate lust is to prefer selfish desire to selfless love.

Lust also destroys marriages; love binds them. Fidelity to one's spouse is a sign of faithfulness to God. Today the churches must wrestle with the problem of divorce because half of marriages fail. Many denominations permit Christian marriage after divorce if it can be proven that the original marriage bond was defective in some way—that one or both partners entered matrimony only conditionally, or imposed restrictions on their mutual love and support. In effect, the churches make the judgment that true marriage was never entered into in the first instance.

Lust is a shallow substitute for love, which above all motivates the disciple. Although Jesus appears to prescribe harsh remedies, he does not seriously suggest self-mutilation or even celibacy. Rather, his message is to deny the temptation at its source. As Jesus gave up his body to us in death, we are to dedicate our bodies to him in life.

One caution is in order here. There is a danger that disciples will deny their senses to the point of obsession. Through the centuries, in fact, scrupulous Christians have mortified the flesh by flagellation. For example, Thomas More and Blaise Pascal wore hairshirts. Such practices typically produce the opposite effect of what Jesus intended—a focus on lust. Jesus wanted his disciples to get outside of themselves to love God and serve neighbor, not to be self-absorbed. Ultimately, lust is a form of selfishness that puts one's own interests central, while discounting the fact that the other is a child of God.

A Plain "Yes" or "No" (Matthew 5:33-37)

> "Again, you have heard that the people in the old days were told—'Thou shalt not forswear thyself, but shalt perform unto the Lord thine oaths,' but I say to you, don't use an oath at all. Don't swear by Heaven for it is God's throne, nor by the earth for it is his footstool, nor by Jerusalem for it is the city of the great king. No, and don't swear by your own head, for you cannot make a single hair—white or black! Whatever you have to say let your 'yes' be a plain 'yes' and your 'no' a plain 'no'—anything more than this has a taint of evil."

It is ironic, in view of Jesus' teaching against oaths, that Christians today swear on a *Bible* to tell "the truth, the whole truth, and nothing but the truth." But the practice, at least as we understand it today, serves a purpose. Our hand on the Bible doesn't guarantee the truthfulness of our words, but it serves to generate an atmosphere of gravity to our testimony. When our truthfulness is likely to affect the life of another, we must not offer our words lightly. The Bible is a powerful symbol of truth in our culture. Most mainstream churches accept the practice as necessary to ensure justice in civil and criminal cases. Quakers and other small sects, however, adhere strictly to Jesus' prohibition, and courts have accommodated their members. Saint Augustine noted that the pagan philosophers believed oaths were beneath the dignity of gentlemen. For Christians, an oath is a call on God himself to affirm one's truthfulness and avenge the liar. An oath protests innocence: "May God strike me dead if I am not telling the truth!"

But experience amply demonstrates that, were God to strike every liar dead, no one would be left on earth. On occasion, all of us withhold the "whole" truth to protect ourselves from improper questions or to spare the feelings of others. Sincerity is no virtue when we justify its use to diminish others. When the truth hurts, charity must prevail, and we must hold our tongues.

Jesus' message is positive: keep your promises and be faithful to your word. Be truthful even when the personal cost is great. Jesus was truthful when the High Priest insisted, "I command you by the living God, to tell us on your oath if you are Christ, the Son of God." Forced to answer under oath, Jesus' truthfulness got him killed.

To be sure, eliminating oaths altogether will not guarantee that the truth will be told. Moreover, Jesus' disciples must be careful not to swear to more than they know or to a future commitment they do not fully understand. Christians are bound to God's will alone, not to a court or paper contract. What Jesus seeks is not just true words from our mouths, but truth in our hearts, truth lived in the daily details of our lives. That truth will make us free.

RETALIATION (MATTHEW 5:38–42)

"You have heard that it used to be said 'An eye for an eye and a tooth for a tooth,' but I tell you, don't resist evil. If a man hits your right cheek, turn the other one to him as well. If a man wants to sue you for your coat, let him have it and your cloak as well. If anybody forces you to go a mile with him, do more—go two miles with him. Give to the man who asks anything from you, and don't turn away from the man who wants to borrow."

Later in the sermon, Jesus will bid his disciples to "treat other people exactly as you would like to be treated by them," adding that "this is the essence of all true religion" (Matthew 7:12). The Golden Rule, of course, presumes that it is *good* treatment we are reciprocating. Here, though, Jesus counsels his disciples on how to respond to *ill* treatment.

In the old covenant every evil was meant to be answered in kind, with the understanding that retribution would overcome evil. Jesus, however, says that the right way to requite evil is not to resist it. As Bonhoeffer explains: "The only way to overcome evil is to let it run itself to a standstill because it does not find the resistance it is looking for."

As Mohandas Gandhi and Martin Luther King, Jr., demonstrated, nonviolence exposes evildoers for what they are. When churches were set ablaze, dogs set upon defenseless people, and water cannons used to disperse marchers and crowds during the civil rights demonstrations of the 1960s, the world was enraged at the white supremacists, not just because the evil was one-sided, but because peace was being violated by the savage ugliness of violence.

When Jesus counsels his disciples to endure evil, he does not mean that evil enjoys rights. In his sermon he calls persecutors wicked, but he asks his disciples to better expose the evil by doing *more* than their persecutors demand—to walk another mile, to give another coat, to turn the other cheek. Expose the bullies for what they are: cowards who must hide their fear behind displays of false power!

Of course, only a utopian society could be based on such defenselessness. Jesus knows the world is evil and that weakness attracts aggression. Thus, he makes no pretense of offering a social blueprint. Nor does he deny the

secular authority the right and responsibility to resist evil
and defend people. His point is that his kingdom is not of
this world. Because his disciples are already citizens of
heaven, they must act by heaven's rules. It is their *personal*
behavior that Jesus is prescribing, knowing full well that
they will suffer abuse this side of eternity.

ENEMIES (MATTHEW 5:43–48)

"You have heard that it used to be said, 'Thou shalt
love thy neighbor and hate thine enemy,' but I tell
you, Love your enemies, and pray for those who
persecute you, so that you may be sons of your
Heavenly Father. For he makes his sun rise upon
evil men as well as good, and he sends his rain upon
honest and dishonest men alike. For if you love only
those who love you, what credit is that to you? Even
tax-collectors do that! And if you exchange greetings only with your own circle, are you doing anything exceptional? Even the pagans do that much.
No, you are to be perfect, like your Heavenly
Father."

In the sermon, this is Jesus' first mention of *love*—the
defining characteristic of the Christian. Love—the love of a
disciple of Jesus—is neither sentiment nor sentimentality
nor passion nor even response to affection. Rather, Christian love is concern for those who hate us. The implication
is clear: that we are to care for our enemies because God
loves all of his creatures without distinction. In this respect
of loving all, we emulate God himself.

It is not enough to turn our own hatred into love, but to
love those who hate us, without any guarantee that our love
will conquer their enmity. Where hatred can be overcome, it
will only be by calling on love. Mere nonresistance is inad-
equate in the face of abuse; we must love our persecutors.

The context of the sermon serves to explain this
extraordinary demand. The Jews of Jesus' time considered
God to be their possession—exclusively. When called to
love their neighbors, they restricted their caring to other
Jews; all others they considered to be real or potential

enemies, deserving of their enmity. The Israelites, in fact, considered their wars to be holy because they were fighting for *their* God against godless and corrupt strangers. Now, Jesus proclaims a new understanding: all peoples are God's people. To love your neighbor means to love every neighbor, even those who hate you—Jew and Gentile alike. Since God makes no distinctions, there are no distinctions.

Remember that, while Jesus is addressing the multitudes, he is speaking of his disciples, who cannot help but encounter the same hatred that will be heaped on Jesus himself. Practically speaking, it is impossible for Jesus' followers to do good while motivated by hatred for the very persons they are trying to help. The only possible motive for the disciples' mission is love. John Stott suggests that it is still possible to hate *God's* enemies, so long as we do not hate our own. But how can we determine who God's adversaries are?

History amply illustrates that Christians have sought to justify their own wars and persecutions by pretending to vindicate their God. In the two world wars of the last century, for example, there were Christian chaplains tending to the spiritual needs of soldiers on *both sides of the conflict*. That should give us pause. Surely God is not "on" or "for" one side or the other. In the love of one's enemies, there is no self-righteousness, there is no right and wrong, there are no bad guys and good guys. Love of one's oppressors is not a feeling, but a concern. We care for our enemies because they belong to God, they are loved by God, and they have the same destiny as we.

Can we emulate Jesus in this regard, becoming perfect like his Father? Yes. In his recent commentary on the sermon, professor of the New Testament, Dale C. Allison, notes that by "perfection" Jesus cannot mean sinlessness. We still must seek God's forgiveness. Rather, it means *completeness*—an integrity of life consistent with the Beatitudes. Although complete in this respect, disciples must continue to "hunger and thirst" for goodness and ask forgiveness for their shortcomings.

When enemies are loved, then *everyone* is loved; no creature is unloved in God's kingdom. "The man who does not love cannot know [God] at all, for God is love" (1 John 4:8).

GOODNESS IN OBSCURITY (MATTHEW 6:1–4)

> "Beware of doing your good deeds conspicuously to catch men's eyes or you will miss the reward of your Heavenly Father. So, when you do good to other people, don't hire a trumpeter to go in front of you—like those play-actors in the synagogues and streets who make sure that men admire them. Believe me, they have had all the reward they are going to get! No, when you give to charity, don't even let your left hand know what your right hand is doing, so that your giving may be secret. Your Father, who knows all secrets, will reward you."

For periods in our professional lives, my wife and I have taken on responsibilities as fund-raisers for nonprofit and charitable organizations. It's our experience that careers in "financial development" (a transparent euphemism) tend to attract men and women with warm hearts and thick skins. Like telemarketers, fund-raisers suffer more failures than they enjoy successes. But unlike telemarketers, they have no products to sell—only causes. Not surprisingly, prospective givers are elusive, resistant, and sometimes insulting to those who solicit their generosity.

Many people who "give to charity" demand something in return, usually in the form of public acknowledgment of their philanthropy. If they give substantial sums, they expect their name to be placed on a building, carved into a wall, or etched on a scroll. If they are wealthy enough to make philanthropy a regular practice, they might even create charitable foundations bearing their names, thus informing the whole world of their generosity. Jesus, however, prefers the anonymous and spontaneous giver. It is the way he operated himself, typically cautioning the men and women he cured to tell no one about it.

We must not lose sight of what appears to be a contradiction at this point. Recall that earlier in his sermon, Jesus told his disciples to be a light to the world; clearly, this would call for goodness and justice that can be witnessed by others. Now Jesus seems to contradict himself by telling them to do good in obscurity. This obscurity is not a hiding from the eyes of the world, but a hiding from our own self-congratulatory eyes. Our giving must not be for our own satisfaction in watching ourselves do something good. Rather, our good work must become such a habit that it is neither self-serving nor contrived, but natural, almost unconscious. As Bonhoeffer notes: "Genuine love is always self-forgetful in the true sense of the world."

During the Great Depression, the comedian Fred Allen used to fill his pockets with quarters every morning and distribute them to anyone who asked or seemed needy— even professional beggars. Allen did not boast of his generosity, however; to our knowledge he didn't even reflect on it. When his pockets were empty, he simply filled them again.

Professional fund-raisers promise prospective donors that they will feel gratified by their decision to be generous, and that they will be recognized. Jesus, by contrast, preaches that generosity to the needy is not an option but a responsibility. Like other duties, it must be dispatched without fanfare—especially from ourselves. God promises to match our generosity many times over.

Questions to Ponder

1. Compare the community in which you live with the world community. How does your condition compare with the lives of others?

2. What is your responsibility to those less fortunate than you?

3. How does the good news of the gospel improve the human condition?

4. How can you make Jesus known to others without being heavy-handed and unwelcome?

5. How can you be sincere without telling hurtful truths?

Following in Jesus' Steps

1. *Truth-telling.* On occasion, Jesus was evasive when challenged. When might it be permissible for me to stop short of revealing the whole truth?

2. *Anger.* Jesus was sometimes angry. When can I be angry?

3. *Lust.* How do I cultivate a love life without being lustful?

4. *Going the extra mile.* Practically and personally speaking, what must I do to love my enemies?

5. *Generosity.* In my own life, what can I do to be more generous?

The Big Question

How can I be salt of the earth and light to the world?

THREE

"And Whenever You Pray ..."

Concerning Prayer

(Matthew 6:5–15)

"And then, when you pray, don't be like the play-actors. They love to stand and pray in the synagogues and at street-corners so that people may see them at it. Believe me, they have had all the reward they are going to get. But when you pray, go into your own room, shut your door, and pray to your Father privately. Your Father, who sees all private things, will reward you. And when you pray, don't rattle off long prayers like the pagans who think they will be heard because they use so many words. Don't be like them. For your Father knows your needs before you ask him" (Matthew 6:5–8).

The greeting card industry in the United States makes millions of dollars each year compensating for our inability to express ourselves to the people we care about.

"How do I love thee? Let me count the ways ... " Why should I attempt the composition of a personal love letter when Elizabeth Barrett Browning has already done it better and is no longer around to object to my borrowing her words? I do not mind leaning on the anonymous authors who compose greetings for Hallmark and Ambassador to express how I feel about weddings, anniversaries, births, illness, death, graduation, promotion—about my parents, children, and secretary, and about Christmas, Easter, and even St. Patrick's Day.

Our lack of courage in expressing our sentiments is in sharp contrast with past centuries. For example, walking through an eighteenth-century cemetery not far from my home, I am always struck by the inscriptions on the tombstones of persons long gone. Here, etched in worn stone, are the brief but poignant profiles of devoted mothers, faithful fathers, loving children, and generous citizens. And then, of course, there were those masters of the nineteenth century who could dash off a work of art to fit the occasion. There was Richard Wagner who drafted *Siegfried Idyll* to honor the birth of his son, and Claude Debussy who composed the *Children's Corner Suite* to amuse his young child. People then simply were not afraid to express themselves.

When my own children were small we spent our annual vacations in homes exchanged with other families. One summer, on holiday to Connecticut, we came upon an heirloom of our host family—a register from the nineteenth century signed by relatives, guests, and neighbors over many years. The album was filled with penned appreciations by adults and children, sweetly (and I suspect honestly) expressing the value they placed on love, friendship, and gratitude. All were sentiments written by very ordinary people, but by today's greeting-card standards, they were in a class with Elizabeth Barrett Browning.

Improvisation in Prayer

I do not altogether regret that this year, once again, I will choose a greeting card and sentiment for my wife's birthday identical to that selected by tens of thousands of other American husbands. It is a reminder that I am neither the center of the universe nor the world's greatest lover. Were I to summon the courage to write my wife a love letter in lieu of sending a commercial card, the product of my labor would in any event bear a close resemblance to the efforts of other uxorious American males in advanced middle age.

The pioneering photographer Ernst Haas, who looked at life through a camera, concluded: "Each man on earth is nothing but a mosaic of a picture he will never see." You and I indeed are but pieces of a big picture, and our thoughts and sentiments, while they are ours, are not unique. Viewed from that perspective, the improvisation of emotion is pretentious, whereas formulas, by contrast, offer some dependability. The articulate American Lutheran theologian Martin Marty acknowledges that he is not at all adept at improvising prayer, and thus he looks to the wisdom and artful expressions of others:

> I'm not a prayerful genius like the religious philosopher and scientist Pascal. I am not even someone who could edit and expound Pascal. But I can read him prayerfully, and the thoughts he inspires will convey me to different levels of being, to new depths. So I spend a lot of time with anthologies of prayers, with quotations, sourcebooks . . . and so on. Whether all those trips produce the language of "I" and "Thou" I'm not sure, but I am a book person, and therefore if I draw close to God, it is likely to be through reading (*USA Weekend*, December 25, 1994).

Ultimately, prayer is a love letter to God—and granted, it is not easy to compose, just as it is not easy to love. Love "at first sight" is rare and suspect. Love takes learning; devotion takes practice. So does discipleship. One might imagine that the twelve men who lived closest to Jesus would have found it easy to express themselves to him. The Gospels confirm the contrary. Jesus' friends were, if anything, even more emotionally tongue-tied than we are. But they didn't fake a facility they lacked. Rather, they humbly asked Jesus, "Teach us to pray"—and he complied. Here is Jesus' response in its less familiar J. B. Phillips translation:

> "Our Heavenly Father, may your name be honoured;
> May your kingdom come, and your will be done on earth as it is in Heaven.
> Give us each day the bread we need for the day,
> Forgive us what we owe to you, as we have also forgiven those who owe anything to us.
> Keep us clear of temptation, and save us from evil"
> (Matthew 6:9–13).

Christians have the Lord's Prayer, often called the Our Father, committed to memory in its standard, ritual translation. Encoded in our gray matter, it rests waiting to be summoned as automatically (and mindlessly) as the pledge of allegiance and the first verse of our national anthem. In any ritual, religious or secular, familiarity does not necessarily breed contempt, but it can numb our comprehension of the words.

The Lord's Prayer, although it is ancient, is not at all quaint; rather, it is practical, comprehensive, up to date, and, in its own way, no less radical than the Beatitudes. While the prayer stands by itself, it is a continuation of Jesus' Sermon on the Mount and recapitulates his message. Unfortunately, the very familiarity of the prayer has diminished its power. Thus it bears analysis to restore the meaning the original disciples found in it as the answer to their question, and ours: "How are we to pray?" To take a close look at the Lord's Prayer, however, we must enter the prayer fully and let the familiar words regain the force of their original meaning. In effect, we must explore each key phrase of the prayer to understand the depth of Jesus' meaning for his disciples—then and now.

"OUR FATHER" (MATTHEW 6:9)

Jesus invites us to address God as he does—as a loving parent. Not simply as Creator but as a *relative*—everyone's Father. From the very outset, Jesus is suggesting something new and unfamiliar. Brazenly, Jesus says to his disciples, "This is *our* God—not privately *mine* or privately *yours*, but *ours*, and *we* are his." This redefines religion. Despite its predilection to personify its deities, pagan religion never came close to depicting God in terms of a loving and caring family relationship.

Jesus is uniquely God's Son, but we are also God's children by adoption—and Jesus' brothers and sisters in the flesh. Moreover, we are made in God's image, partaking of his nature. While Jesus alone can affirm that "the Father and I are one," he summons us to "be perfect as my Heavenly Father is perfect." Jesus could not offer such an invitation were we not also children of his Father. As Bonhoeffer notes, "In the name of the Son of God [the disciples] are privileged to call God Father."

When I was writing my first book, *Growing in Faith*, I was cautioned by a friend who is a seminary president to make the references in my text gender-neutral: to choose "humanity" or "humankind" over "mankind"; to employ "one" instead of "him" when referring to an individual who could be either a woman or a man; and to stress God's "parenthood" rather than God's "fatherhood." Such reconstruction of language is not as easy as it sounds and, even when successful, makes for awkward prose. Moreover, when taken too literally, gender correctness distorts reality.

The fatherhood of God, while stressed by Jesus, certainly is consistent in the history of Judaism. In the story of the Exodus from Egypt, for example, God instructed Moses to tell Pharaoh, "This is what Yahweh says: 'Israel is my firstborn son'" (Exodus 4:22). The prophet Hosea expressed the tenderness of the parental relationship: "When Israel was a child I loved him, and out of Egypt I called my son . . . it was I who taught Ephraim to walk, I took (my people) in my arms . . . and I bent down to them and fed them" Hosea 11:1, 3–4).

God's parenthood is so all-embracing that Jesus, in hyperbole, warns us against comparing any merely human relationship to it: "Don't call any human being 'father'— for you have one Father and he is in heaven" (Matthew 23:9). Saint Paul underscores the fact: "It is because you really are his sons that God has sent the Spirit of his Son into your hearts to cry, 'Father, dear Father.' You, my brother, are not a servant any longer; you are a son. And, if you are a son, then you are certainly an heir of God through Christ" (Galatians 4:6–7).

The Lord's Prayer is intended by Jesus to be recited in the company of others. It addresses God as "*our* Father," not as exclusively "*my* Father." You and I share him with everyone else, alive, deceased, or yet to be born. While God possesses you and me, we do not have exclusive rights to him. It is the nature of siblings to compete for parental affection, but God does not play favorites. As we know from Jesus' parables, the stray sheep and the prodigal son are as precious to God as a faithful son and daughter.

Christianity is a radically democratic religion, with equal rights and privileges for all—as co-heirs with Jesus of an eternal glory in which we shall amazingly "share in God's essential nature" (2 Peter 1:4).

"WHO ART IN HEAVEN" (MATTHEW 6:9)

Because we believe that God knows and sees everything, we assume he must have a vantage point to view his universe, as the Greek gods had on Mount Olympus. "God is watching!" we tell a mischievous child. Of course, none of us really believes in a three-tiered universe (heaven "up there," hell "down there," and us in the middle), but this myth from childhood dies hard. What do we have to replace it?

A millennium before Jesus walked the earth, King Solomon affirmed that "the heavens and their own heavens cannot contain God" (1 Kings 8:27). The psalmist agreed:

> If I climb up into heaven, thou art there;
> if I go down to hell, thou art there also.
> If I take the wings of the morning,
> and remain in the uttermost parts of the sea;
> even there also shall thy hand lead me,
> and thy right hand shall hold me (Psalm 139:8–10).

Although God is everywhere, he is not just coextensive with his own universe, because that would give him dimensions. Heaven is clearly not a *place* at all, but a perfection. The late English Jesuit Thomas Corbishley suggested that we are safer rendering "heavenly" as "unearthly." The perfection of God is everything those of us on earth are not. He is immaterial, not spread across space but present in every place.

The poet Robert Browning was mocked for proclaiming that "God's in his heaven, all's right with the world." His critics recognized rightly that the world wants for perfection, and so do we. But to give the poet his due, Browning was referring to providence. He knew that God is capable of making our crooked paths straight, even when we cannot.

If heaven is literally inconceivable, God's kingdom is nonetheless palpable for those who would be Jesus' disciples. The Spirit of God already makes his home in our individual hearts, minds, and bodies, where he strains to realize the kingdom within us. So the disciple will look for God not in some distant heaven but in his or her inner kingdom.

"HALLOWED BE THY NAME" (MATTHEW 6:9)

Why hallow God's *name* when we ought to praise God for himself? That is certainly our contemporary way of thinking, but the Lord's Prayer reflects ancient ways. While you and I think of names only as convenient but arbitrary labels, the ancients endowed words with a significance that gave them an almost independent reality.

In his Gospel, St. John refers to God's Son as the *Word* uttered by God from all eternity, which became incarnate in Jesus: "So the Word of God became a human being and lived among us" (John 1:14). In the Old Testament, God changes Abram's name to Abraham, signifying that he is now "the father of nations." Likewise Jesus gives Simon the Apostle a new name—Peter—the "rock" on which he will build his church.

There is power in naming things. Scientists name stars and elements for their colleagues; explorers and politicians name whole nations for themselves. We give names to our children and our pets. (Our twin cats are named Fred and Ginger, because they move as gracefully as Astaire and Rogers.) In the Genesis story, the first man and woman assert their dominion over all the creatures in Eden by assigning them their names.

Lofty personages take their names seriously and use their names in specialized ways. The woman Elizabeth II will always be compared with Elizabeth I because she bears the same name. A few years ago, a guard at the Tower of London corrected my wife when she asked a question about "Elizabeth the Great." He replied testily, "Our present queen is also great!" When another British queen, Victoria, pronounced, "*We* are not amused," she was referring to herself not as an individual like you or me, but as an institution. This recalls Richard Nixon, who in later years referred to his past prominence in the third person: "When *Nixon* was president of the United States and leader of the free world . . . " In each instance the careful use of names by individuals both exalts and protects their persons.

God has long since revealed his name: Yahweh—*I am who am*. In deference to the deity, Judaism makes every effort *not* to address God by his proper name but rather to use substitutes such as "Lord" or "Holy One." If you are like me, you resent total strangers presuming to call you by your first name until you have become better acquainted and permit familiarity. To hallow God's name is to affirm that he is holy, set apart, sacred, and unique. It is unwise in any case to get too cozy with God; although we bear his image, we are not exactly in his league.

As a journalist, I find use of the passive voice anathema even in prayer, and I avoid it at any cost if possible. However, to rewrite Jesus' prayer in the active voice, we would have to say "*We* hallow thy name." As C. S. Lewis remarks, you and I would be pretending that we mortals are the only ones praising God, whereas in fact we are joined by countless angels and all creation in a chorus of praise.

"THY KINGDOM COME" (MATTHEW 6:10)

That is, may God's reign, with its beauty and peace, extend over our lives here, in our hearts and in all the places we inhabit. In an age of democracy, we think of government in terms of elective politics, which is the conflict of counterbalancing forces. In the past, however, a good monarch concentrated his or her time not on campaigning and competing for votes but on securing peace and prosperity. That is what we have in mind in God's kingdom.

I am reminded of Edward Hicks's painting, *The Peaceable Kingdom*, in which the lion is lying down with the lamb and is no more threatening than a tabby cat. Hicks's recreation of Eden may be fanciful, but peace is a social and personal reality. It is not simply the absence of turmoil but the fulfillment of our natures. Let us not forget to pray also for the dead, that God's kingdom may also come to them. When loved ones die we sensibly pray that they may have a "perfect rest"—not that they be cocooned for eternity, but that they become citizens of God's peaceable kingdom.

Father Corbishley recalls instances in the Old Testament where men attributed a harshness to God that masked their own responsibilities to confirm his kingdom. For example, claiming that God "hardened Pharaoh's heart" (Exodus 4:21; 7:3) to persecute the Jews makes God the heavy, whereas, in fact, Pharaoh needed no encouragement whatsoever to act tyrannically. If God is not a democrat, neither is he a tyrant. His kingdom is altruistic, peaceable, loving, and compassionate.

What are we to make of Jesus' claim that the kingdom is already here? Why pray for what we already possess? Because only the seeds of the kingdom are in our hearts. Individuals have been redeemed, not society. With the urging of the Spirit within, Jesus' disciples affirm and realize the kingdom of God among all creatures.

"THY WILL BE DONE" (MATTHEW 6:10)

C. S. Lewis cautions us not to submit passively to God's wishes, nor to assume that God's will for us is replete with trials and disappointments to be endured. In fact, it is insulting to God's graciousness just to hunker down for life's inevitable disappointments, thanking him only for the occasional blessing. God's will for us is much more generous than we imagine. Perhaps we can better understand this by looking at the Third World's developing nations. Formerly subject peoples possess what political scientists term "rising expectations," an awareness that their quality of life can be improved and a willingness to work toward that. Like the populations of the Third World, we know what good is available to us, and we are willing to do what it takes to participate in that goodness. In the long run, what we are requesting is that God give us "the same mind that was also in Christ"—to take on the motivation of the one person who always followed God's will. "My food is doing the will of him who sent me and finishing the work he has given me" (John 4:34). Jesus' obedience to God's will brought about our redemption. By imitating him we collaborate in the full realization of the kingdom.

Brother Ramon, a contemporary Anglican lay hermit, prays for God's will in this poignant way:

> Have your own way, Lord, have your own way,
> You are the potter, I am the clay;
> Mold me and make me after your will,
> As I am waiting, yielded and still.

"On earth as it is in heaven" (Matthew 6:10)

What would a kingdom be like where God's will is done? Here is Scripture's attempt to depict the new heaven and new earth:

> Violence will no longer be heard of in your country,
>   not devastation and ruin within your frontiers . . .
> Nor more will the sun give daylight,
>   nor moonlight shine upon you,
> but Yahweh will be your everlasting light.
>   Your God will be your splendor (Isaiah 60:18–19).

Saint John exults:

> See! The home of God is with men,
> and he will live among them.
> They shall be his people,
> and God himself shall be with them,
> and will wipe away every tear from their eyes.
> Death shall be no more,
> and never again shall there be crying or pain . . .
> See! I am making all things new . . . I will give to the
> thirsty water without price from the fountain of life
> . . . The city has no need for the light of the sun or
> moon, for the splendor of God fills it with light and
> its radiance is the Lamb (Revelation 21:3–6, 23).

If this apocalyptic description falls short of satisfying us, it at least suggests that the kingdom is a surprise and certainly not a bore.

But the kingdom cannot be realized without our active collaboration. During much of the last century the Social Gospel movement aimed specifically to encourage Christians to build God's kingdom on earth through peace, social justice, and the elimination of sickness and poverty. The popes equally urged the faithful to make life on earth a mirror of the justice, tranquility, and love that prevail in the kingdom of heaven.

The disciple is a light to the *world*, the salt of the *earth*— a citizen of the heavenly kingdom, to be sure, but a laborer working to make the world what God intended it to be when he created paradise as our original home. The earth was made for us. It is our obligation to make it right again.

"GIVE US THIS DAY OUR DAILY BREAD" (MATTHEW 6:11)

Jesus' redundancy here bears significance. Faithful disciples are not hoarders, stockpiling necessities against a rainy day, like some 1950s householder provisioning his bomb shelter against a nuclear holocaust. Rather, disciples ask God for what is sufficient to get them through this day alone. Remember that the Lord's Prayer emerges from the Sermon on the Mount, where Jesus speaks of the lilies of the field. He is telling his disciples not to be greedy out of anxiety for tomorrow, but to ask humbly for what they need and for what their brothers and sisters need, and nothing more.

Recovering alcoholics live by the rule "One day at a time," realizing that it is the best they can manage in the trial to remain sober. Most of us, however, are brought up to believe that we must secure our futures today by planning for tomorrow's every contingency. All my insurance policies are contrivances to cushion me from future disaster. Of course, God is our ultimate insurance policy. He also supplies our present needs, which are really the only ones we have, because we have no alternative but to live in the present.

To ask for today's necessities *today* puts a realistic edge on our prayer. But once we get started, we are tempted to meander in our devotions and to seek God's help with our psyches, our jobs, our looks, our love lives, and other cosmic, long-range concerns. Prayer can easily become dreamy and speculative when it takes on the big picture. Better that we admit we are hungry now and rely on God for today's rations.

Two final observations are worth noting at this point. First, when we are hungry, it is a solitary need; we do not feel the hunger of others. Yet, Jesus tells us to pray for *our* daily bread—to satisfy *our* common necessities. Every 3.6 seconds around the world someone dies of hunger; 75 percent of them are children. One of every five children in the United States goes to bed hungry every night. What are we to do? We are to do what Jesus would do: we must satisfy their hunger. We will always have the poor among us, and our efforts to feed them and meet their needs must be consistent and authentic.

Second, Jesus acknowledged that human beings do not live by bread alone (see Matthew 4:4), meaning there are other acute needs we rely on for our overall well-being. Perhaps we think we need a new job or a new spouse when we really need a vacation or an extra hour of sleep each night. This wisdom is part of the "daily bread" Jesus' disciples pray for.

"FORGIVE US OUR TRESPASSES AS WE FORGIVE THOSE WHO TRESPASS AGAINST US" (MATTHEW 6:12)

This is the nub of it—the hardest thing to do, yet the most reasonable. How can we expect God to forgive us if we do not forgive others?

But how it goes against the grain—and how we contrive to avoid situations where we might have an enemy to forgive! Ever since you and I graduated from a childhood in which disputes were settled by fists, we have inhabited a world of adults who studiously avoid confrontation. This avoidance of antagonizing people we dislike is less a reflection of kindliness and more a realization that, should we make an enemy, we must then either sustain our hostility or forgive him. Neither is an appetizing option.

I suspect that the key is understanding what forgiving is all about. By forgiving, we let go of the enmity that festers in us, even when those we are forgiving have no interest in our forgiveness and show no remorse. When we nurture hatred we burden ourselves, becoming in a sense our own enemies. When Jesus forgave his executioners from the cross, they took no notice. But his act of forgiveness freed Jesus to cry, "Father, I commend my spirit into your hands," uncompromised and fully at peace with himself and the world he thereby redeemed.

In perhaps the most arduous step toward sobriety, recovering alcoholics must personally apologize to everyone they harmed during the years they were drinking. Why? What possible good can apologies accomplish after the harm is done and long past? After all, old loves and friendships often cannot be restored. Yet, in the act of asking and giving forgiveness, addicts sense a palpable weight lifted from their lives and a modicum of peace restored. By forgiving others, we not only permit God to forgive us: we manage to forgive ourselves.

Early in the twentieth century, the French aristocrat Charles de Foucauld returned to the Sahara, where he had served as a cavalry officer. He came this time not as a warrior but as a solitary determined to emulate Jesus' own prayerful life in the desert. Foucauld was murdered by tribesmen who were jealous of his moral influence, but the hermit knew what it meant to forgive and seek forgiveness. He prayed:

> Father, forgive me. With my whole soul I see how horrible are my sins to you, how they disgust and insult you, and what a price your Son had to pay to redeem me from them. I realize how much pain I have caused you; and in that realization I feel pain myself, crying with remorse at what I have done. At the same time I recognize that I have no right to ask your forgiveness for my sins unless I forgive others their sins. And, of course, the sins which others commit against me are nothing compared with the sins I have committed against you. Thus in truth I am asking that all mankind might be forgiven (*Oxford Book of Prayers*).

"Lead us not into temptation, but deliver us from evil" (Matthew 6:13)

This is yet another of those ancient expressions that ascribes all power to God while leaving the impression that God might actually choose to place us in harm's way. Rather, we are asking that he protect us from situations in which we might be harmed or be tempted to harm others. Ultimately, we are responsible for ourselves; that is the blessing (as well as the price) of being free. Yet, life is filled with trials and tests. At one point St. Paul asked to be relieved of one of them—"a thorn in my flesh," he called it. But God answered him by leaving the thorn there: "My grace is enough for you: for where there is weakness, my power is shown the more completely" (2 Corinthians 12:9). This led Paul to reassure the Corinthians from his own experience:

> No temptation has come your way that is too hard for flesh and blood to bear. But God can be trusted not to allow you to suffer any temptation beyond your powers of endurance. He will see to it that every temptation has its way out, so that it will be possible for you to bear it (1 Corinthians 10:13).

For the prayerful disciple, the "strength that comes from weakness" is steadfastness in humility. Lacking faith, the world regards Christ on his cross as life's loser. Through faith we know better. From such weakness will be created the new heaven and the new earth, and the promise of eternity with God.

Amen

The Lord's Prayer is the most familiar part of Jesus' sermon and the one that Christians commit to memory from childhood, but with the addition of a concluding word: "Amen." This one word signifies our confidence that God will acknowledge our petitions, and it entrusts us individually and corporately to the Father of us all.

Questions to Ponder

1. How can you make the Lord's Prayer your own personal prayer?

2. Prayer is a love letter to God. How can you use prayer to bring about an increase in love?

3. What is it about God that makes him our Father?

4. The poet proclaimed that "God's in his heaven; all's well with the world." Is that true? Explain.

5. What are we asking for when we pray, "Thy kingdom come"?

Following in Jesus' Steps

1. *Thy will be done.* What is God's will for me? What is his will for the world?

2. *Thy kingdom come.* What can I do to make the world more like God's kingdom?

3. *Give us our daily bread.* How can I simplify my life to become more appreciative of God's simple gifts?

4. *Forgive our trespasses.* How can I admit my faults while still striving to follow Jesus?

5. *Lead us not into temptation.* What can I do to avoid faltering?

The Big Question

How can I make my life a prayer?

FOUR

"AND WHENEVER YOU FAST ..."

CONCERNING FASTING
(MATTHEW 6:16–34)

According to Dietrich Bonhoeffer:

> Jesus takes it for granted that his disciples will observe the pious custom of fasting. Strict exercise of self-control is an essential feature of the Christian's life. Such customs have only one purpose—to make the disciples more ready and cheerful to accomplish those things which God would have done.

Three of every five Americans are overweight; one-third of that number are actually obese. Our national fixation with losing weight feeds a diet industry that absorbs $34 *billion* every year. America is the true land of milk and honey, and we consume too much of it. Paradoxically, we invest our wealth in loss rather than gain.

The reason we spend vast sums on dieting is because the only effective alternative—fasting—is unpleasant. It means doing without. To those who blame obesity on their hormones, scientists note that there were no overweight inmates in Auschwitz.

Jesus continues his Sermon on the Mount with telling his followers not *when* to fast but *how* to fast. The practice of fasting is common to all major religions, not for weight loss but as a discipline of purification, a remedy for self-indulgence, and a means to favor the spirit over the flesh.

Fasting is so much a part of daily living that we call the first meal of the day "break-fast."

In Jesus' time, the Pharisees fasted twice a week, on Tuesdays and Thursdays. Daily, John the Baptist subsisted on what little nourishment he could find in the wilderness. Jesus himself embarked on his ministry only after having fasted forty days and nights in the desert.

The Pharisees compared Jesus unfavorably to the Baptist, because Jesus dined with sinners and set no rules for his disciples. In his sermon, Jesus assumes that people of faith will fast. In the Lord's Prayer we ask only: "Give us each day the bread we need for the day." But Jesus attacks the pretension of those who would draw attention to their piety by their fasts.

FEAST OR FAMINE (MATTHEW 6:16–18)

> "Then, when you fast, don't look like those miserable play-actors! For they deliberately disfigure their faces so that people may see that they are fasting. Believe me, they have had all their reward. No, when you fast, anoint your head and wash your face so that nobody knows that you are fasting—let it be a secret between you and your Father. And your Father who knows all secrets will reward you."

There are those who lament that life is either feast or famine. Fasting is hardly famine, but it is a self-imposed discipline that sharpens one's senses to appreciate God as Author of our feasts. In the Old Testament, God's people sacrificed animal life to God to affirm that he alone can give life. Fasting conveys the same message, adding a note of gratitude for life and bounty.

Many Christians still follow a calendar of feast days and fast days. Mardi Gras, which has long since become a secular celebration, anticipates the Lenten season of self-denial. Catholics fast before the eucharistic feast. My own Quaker meeting features "simple meals" of soup and bread with a twofold purpose: to acknowledge God's bounty and to share with those who are truly in need.

Jesus approved of fasting but did not make a fetish of it. Like other spiritual disciplines, fasting only "works" if it makes us more appreciative of our blessings. Alternatively, some Christians do without food and drink to punish the flesh. Paul models this for us; after his conversion, he went three days and nights without nourishment as penance for having persecuted Christians. Later, he compared fasting to the discipline an athlete imposes on himself in training.

In the past, fervent Christians flagellated themselves or wore hair shirts as penance, seeking not only to deny and discipline themselves, but to punish the body as if it were their enemy. The danger of such extreme measures is to conceive of the body as evil rather than the temple of God. In practice, self-punishment only emphasizes the flesh, when the disciple is seeking to grow in spirit.

Jesus responded to criticism that his disciples seldom fasted by comparing his presence among them to a wedding feast:

> "Can you expect wedding guests to mourn while they have the bridegroom with them? The day will come when the bridegroom will be taken away from them—they will certainly fast then!" (Matthew 9:15).

Fasting is closely associated with prayer, which is incompatible with self-indulgence. People do not pray with their mouths full. But Jesus' concern is not *when* we fast, but *how* we fast. As John Stott notes:

> Jesus (contrasts) two alternative kinds of piety, pharisaic and Christian. Pharisaic piety is ostentatious, motivated by vanity and reward by men. Christian piety is secret, motivated by humility and rewarded by God. . . . It is only when we are aware of his presence that our giving, praying, and fasting will be real.

Even then, Bonhoeffer warns against self-delusion: "I (can) turn myself into a spectator of my own prayer performance. . . . I can lay on a very nice show for myself even in the privacy of my own room." Disciples must take care to choose God alone as their audience.

Jesus makes it clear that his followers will be rewarded, that they do not accomplish good for its own sake but for the sake of God's kingdom, which, as Dale Allison notes "will be full of disproportionate grace and so surprising. So there can be no calculation of this reward for that act. . . . Because love, which is the basis of reward, is not quantifiable, judgment is not made with a scale of balances."

OUR TREASURE AND OUR HEART (MATTHEW 6:19–21)

> "Don't pile up treasures on earth, where moth and rust can spoil them and thieves can break in and steal. But keep your treasure in Heaven where there is neither moth nor rust to spoil it and nobody can break in and steal. For wherever your treasure is, your heart will be there too!"

Bonhoeffer insisted that "discipleship can only be maintained so long as nothing is allowed to come between Christ and ourselves"—not even religion or personal piety.

That we are to lay up treasures in heaven not on earth is not to denigrate life's pleasures. Rather, earthy goods are to be seen as gifts that are to be savored rather than collected and hoarded. For the wandering Israelites in the desert, God provided manna for sustenance each day. When they began saving it for future needs, however, it became inedible. In the Lord's Prayer, we ask only for today's necessities. To hoard God's blessings is to pretend to possess them as our own. Bonhoeffer calls such self-indulgence *idolatry*.

We do not know how Jesus and his disciples paid for their needs, only that they lived simply and had a common purse. Revealingly, that purse was held by Judas, who betrayed Jesus for thirty pieces of silver. Having chosen money over his Master, Judas despaired and hanged himself.

We *do* know that when Jesus sent out his disciples to cure the sick and spread the good news, he specified that they carry no money, but rely instead on the hospitality of those they helped. "A workman," Jesus assured them, "deserves his wages" (Luke 10:7). Many centuries later, Francis of Assisi required his friars to beg for food and shelter as they spread the same gospel from town to town.

Today, of course, it is the rare Christian who can expect to operate without a source of income. Young Mormons go two-by-two and door-to-door on mission, living simply, but they are financed by their parents or local churches. Still, the principle stands: "Where your heart is, your treasure will be there too."

To be absolutely clear, Jesus nowhere forbids private property, savings, or insurance, nor does he disdain the enjoyment of God's blessings this side of eternity. Paul reinforces Jesus' teaching by making clear that people who fail to provide for their families are worse than unbelievers (see 1 Timothy 5:8). What matters is that the disciple resist greed and self-indulgence, fixing instead on the legitimate needs of those less fortunate.

CLEAR-SIGHTEDNESS (MATTHEW 6:22–23)

> "The lamp of the body is the eye. If your eye is sound, your whole body will be full of light. But if your eye is evil, your whole body will be full of darkness."

The literal blindness of sight offers a good analogy for the experience of faith. My mother, the only child of blind parents, was born with perfect eyesight. From an early age her eyes provided the only sight her parents had. She read to them and shopped for them. When they left their tiny apartment, she was her parents' escort, telling them when traffic lights turned green. Because they could not afford a seeing-eye dog, they relied on a seeing-eye daughter. Later, as an only child myself, I stepped in to be the eyes for my blind grandfather. He had faith in me to steer him safely. His faith took the place of sight.

When Quakers ask for one another's prayers, they request that they "be held in the light," referring to the prologue to John's Gospel:

> In him appeared life and this life was the light of mankind. The light still shines in the darkness and

the darkness has never put it out . . . the true light,
which shines upon every man . . . (John 1:4–5, 9).

The blind live in total darkness, relying on others' eyes.
In faith, the sighted see the light, which is Christ.

Those who can see have the responsibility of walking in
the light. The self-indulgent are blind because they look
only within themselves. In Judaism, a "good eye" meant
generosity (see Proverbs 22:9), the expression of the light
within. Conversely, an "evil eye" is ungenerous, reflecting
an inner darkness.

The context of Jesus' remarks is his continuing contrast between God and money. He asks those who would
follow him: Where is your heart? In Scripture, one's heart
and one's eye are equivalent. To have our heart in the
right place we must fix our eyes on God's treasures, not
our own.

"Where there is no vision, the people perish" (Proverbs
29:18). The danger to disciples is that they will be myopic,
looking inward to their own piety rather than outward to
the needs of others and to the source of their blessings—
and that is to prefer darkness to the light and to perish in
obscurity. It is no wonder that Judaism conceived of hell as
a place of utter darkness. By contrast, Christ's disciples face
life's challenges with their eyes open.

A Life of Integrity (Matthew 6:24)

> "No one can fully serve two masters. He is bound to
> hate one and love the other, or be loyal to one and
> despise the other. You cannot serve both God and
> the power of money."

One of the delights of my life in semiretirement is that
I am no longer accountable to employers. And although I
would like to boast that now I am my "own boss," that is
not quite a true statement. I remain responsible for my
work and to deadlines, audiences, and my television show,
not to mention my family, friends, and pets. Even when I
was president of a foundation and chairman of a seminary,
I was responsible to my colleagues and contributors. In that

sense, I will always be beholden to others. We never escape "masters."

But living with integrity allows us to serve but one master in our service to others. There is wisdom to the injunction "To thine own self be true." That is the way of integrity, but it does not suggest that we can be our own masters, disregarding others—only that we are capable of consistency in our values, our loves, and our behaviors. Disciples are always responsible for themselves, although self-mastery is a discipline never fully achieved. And although conscience serves as a compass, it is not infallible; rather, it points us in the right direction but cannot make our choices for us. For that we need to look to a guide—to a master.

For the Christian, Jesus is master. And although we cannot imitate all that Jesus did, we can emulate the *way* he acted in everyday life. Learn of me, he advised his followers, because I am meek and humble of heart (see Matthew 11:29). Meekness and humility are at odds with contemporary self-assertion, but Jesus had such integrity that he could afford to be unassuming. He was fully masculine, yet intimate with men and women alike, and in touch with his emotions. In the service of others, he served his Father.

At the same time, Jesus displayed an inexhaustible patience with people and was quick to praise them for their faith. He established an immediate intimacy with all sorts of men and women, which prompted them to reveal themselves to him. He held himself aloof from no one. When crowds surged around him hoping to touch the hem of his garment, he did not deter them. Rather, he could integrate his love for God with his love for others. Bonhoeffer called him "the man for others"—the best of friends.

Jesus explains our choice in uncompromising terms: "No one can fully serve two masters." We may object that we could work several jobs and satisfy each employer, or be equally responsible to our work and our family. But Jesus' imagery is one of slave and master. One cannot be equally beholden to two masters at the same time full time.

Perhaps a better analogy is the behavior of those who commit adultery. They profess to care for their spouse and lover equally. In fact, their loyalty is divided, and the only persons they truly love—self-indulgently—are themselves.

The alternative to God is mammon, the Aramaic term for money or wealth. Why is Jesus so critical of money, when it is the necessary currency of philanthropy? Because wealth offers its owners the illusion that they are masters of their fate. More likely they will be wealth's victims: their money will own them. In Eden, where our first parents enjoyed every blessing, Satan tempted them with the one thing they lacked: *independence* from their Creator and Benefactor. "You will be like God," he promised, if they would disobey their creator (Genesis 3:5).

As disciples of Jesus, the money we earn, inherit, or otherwise come by is to be integrated into our lives as a gift, not a possession. It is not an alternative to God. That explains why Jesus and his original disciples shared a common purse, and why the earliest Christians shared everything. Even today the world's problems are not caused by insufficient wealth, but by its hoarding by the rich at the expense of the poor.

FREEDOM FROM ANXIETY (MATTHEW 6:25–26)

> "That is why I say to you, don't worry about living—wondering what you are going to eat or drink, or what you are going to wear. Surely life is more important than food, and the body more important than the clothes you wear."

Quakers are called "peculiar people" and acknowledge that their simplicity baffles other Christians. Instead of wearing their Sunday best for worship, for example, they deliberately dress down. Their meeting houses are typically large, unadorned rooms with hard benches and no organ, altar, or pulpit. Quakers employ no clergy or staff, but manage to do all the maintenance themselves. They make a single contribution toward utilities and supplies once a year. Most of it goes to the needy inside and outside the meeting. Members call one another "Friends;" if any are in need, others come to their assistance. At the meeting my wife and I attend, worship is followed by a free potluck meal, provided by the members.

Not to put too fine a point on it, Jesus exalts a potluck way of life. One doesn't have to embrace Quaker simplicity to ensure a life free of anxiety. With potluck, of course, you don't have a menu to order from. Instead, you eat what's there. It's the perfect antidote for anxiety.

Every Sunday, Friends bring food as well for poor families in the community—canned goods, staples, things that children like and are easy to prepare. I have yet to see a jar of caviar or a bottle of champagne in the offering basket. But delicacies are not what hungry people need or even want, nor do they need to know what the next meal will consist of, but only that it will be there.

Bonhoeffer notes that

> The way to misuse our possessions is to use them as an insurance against the morrow. Anxiety is always directed to the morrow, whereas goods are in the strictest sense meant to be used only for today. By trying to ensure for the next day we are only creating uncertainty today.

Jesus' counsel against worry follows directly from his comparison of God and mammon, of treasures on earth versus those in heaven. Wealth is not only illusory; it is the source of anxiety and distraction. The wealthy are concerned to protect what they have today so they will have it tomorrow—but they know they are vulnerable to loss, so they prefer gated communities, with guards and security systems.

My wife and I tend to drive used cars that look ordinary and are unattractive to thieves. When they are bumped and scraped in supermarket parking lots, we are chagrined but not desolate. Besides, if I could afford a Rolls Royce, where could I park it without feeling anxious? Simple living is an antidote for anxiety; it not only keeps your credit card balance low but ensures that there will be a meal on the table.

As I write, it is early spring and the lawns are covered by robins dutifully seeking and finding worms and grubs. Jesus points to the natural behavior of birds to call us to the same natural being of our selves in a life often riddled with worry:

> "Look at the birds in the sky. They neither sow nor
> reap nor store away in barns, and yet your Heav-
> enly Father feeds them. Aren't you much more
> valuable to him than they are?" (Matthew 6:26)

A bird's lifestyle certainly doesn't appeal to me, but we hear no complaints from the birds. They may be anxious about predators but not about their next meal. Nor are they burdened by regret for the past. Like our other fellow creatures, they are masters at living in the present moment—an accomplishment that you and I yearn for.

Primitive peoples lacked the advantages of the lower animals: no fur or feathers to keep them warm, no claws, talons, or sharp teeth for protection, no ability to burrow or take flight when challenged. Despite these handicaps, they had to kill to feed themselves. They possessed only their wits for protection. Self-consciousness was a mixed blessing, because it gave them memory and anticipation. They could be frightened of the past and the future alike. Over time, civilization ameliorated most of humankind's handicaps, but not its capacity for anxiety. And more than ever before, anxiety is a destructive reality in our lives today.

By his analogies, Jesus does not mean that we are to be blissfully thoughtless about providing for our needs and the needs of those who depend on us. As John Stott suggests, birds themselves instinctively make provisions for the future, "building their nests, laying and incubating their eggs, and feeding their young. Many migrate to warmer climes before the winter . . . and some even store food . . . "

Rather, it is *obsessive* anxiety about the future, not planning for one's security, that Jesus condemns. He chided Lazarus' sister, for example, for being "worried and bothered about providing so many things" (Luke 10:42). And in the parable of the sower, he explained:

"The seed sown among the thorns represents the people who hear the message and go on their way, and with the worries and riches and pleasures of living, the life is choked out of them, and in the end they produce nothing" (Luke 8:14). Paul echoes Jesus' confidence:

> Don't worry over anything whatever; whenever
> you pray tell God every detail of your needs in

thankful prayer, and the peace of God, which sur-
passes human understanding, will keep constant
guard over your hearts and minds as they rest in
Christ Jesus. . . . Now I have everything I want—in
fact I am rich (Philippians 4:6–7, 18).

Paul's was the wealth that is free from anxiety. We can
be equally rich.

WALKING TALL (MATTHEW 6:27)

"Can any of you, however much he worries, make
himself even a few inches taller?"

In Jesus' world, men and women alike wore sandals,
which couldn't accommodate lifts like the elevator shoes
favored by short people today. I was once engaged to a girl
whose older brother was not much taller than her own four
feet, eleven inches. His slight stature so bothered him that
he joined a national organization of short men whose mission was to reassure its members. Its publication revealed
that many prominent and successful men were not strap-
ping six-footers, and it gave advice on how to *walk* tall with
confidence.

Hollywood, too, goes to great lengths to make short
stars appear tall. With Tom Cruise, for example, it's a matter of camera angles and casting him opposite petite
actresses. In an earlier era, Alan Ladd was made to appear
tall by having Sophia Loren stand and walk in a ditch. No
such stratagems were employed with the legendary
Mickey Rooney, however. He made being short a part of his
personality, and he remains a terrier among actors.

Jesus' point is that the pursuit of prestige so that we
might in some way "tower" above others is not only a distraction but is ultimately futile. Confidence is what makes
the disciple walk tall, and God is its source. The story of
Zacchaeus is exemplary:

And here we find a wealthy man called Zacchaeus,
a chief collector of taxes, wanting to see what sort of
person Jesus was. But the crowd prevented him

> from doing so, for he was very short. So he ran
> ahead and climbed into a sycamore tree to get a
> view of Jesus as he was heading that way. When
> Jesus reached the spot, he looked up and said to
> him, "Zacchaeus, hurry up and come down. I must
> be your guest today." So Zacchaeus hurriedly
> climbed down and gladly welcomed him. But the
> bystanders muttered their disapproval, saying,
> "Now he has gone to stay with a real sinner." But
> Zacchaeus himself stood and said to the Lord,
> "Look, sir, I will give half my property to the poor.
> And if I have swindled anybody out of anything I
> will pay him back four times as much." Jesus said to
> him, "Salvation has come to this house today! Zac-
> chaeus is a descendant of Abraham, and it was the
> lost that the Son of Man came to seek—and to save"
> (Luke 19:1–10).

Although Zacchaeus could not add an inch to his stature, Jesus looked up to him.

The Lilies of the Field (Matthew 6:28–30)

> "And why do you worry about clothes? Consider
> how the wild flowers grow. They neither work nor
> weave, but I tell you that even Solomon in all his
> glory was not arrayed like one of these! Now if God
> so clothes the flowers of the field, which are alive
> today and burnt in the stove tomorrow, is he not
> much more likely to clothe you, you "little-faiths"?

Another distraction that is ultimately futile is our pre-occupation with how we dress. In our culture, clothing conveys status. Even our language portrays this. "Blue collar" refers to manual laborers, who in turn call their desk-bound bosses "suits." Priests, soldiers, police officers, nurses, and firefighters wear uniforms to proclaim their professional status.

When sociologist Michael Harrington wrote his classic study of poverty, *The Other America*, he lamented that cloth-ing had become so inexpensive. His point was that heretofore poverty had been apparent by the way the underclass dressed. But by the mid twentieth century the poor had become invisible because they no longer wore rags and patches. One could be homeless and hungry, yet be dressed in casual clothes similar to those worn by the affluent. When my daughters were young and our budget was tight, my family shopped for castoff clothes at consignment stores, and no one could tell the difference.

Still, Americans fret about what they wear because of the status conveyed by designer labels and logos. It is nothing for a teenager today to demand $150 sneakers and $100 T-shirts. The fashion industry exists not to clothe our nakedness or even to make us appear more attractive, but to make us feel important.

Jesus cautions us not to be anxious about what we wear, because clothing is not permanent. The flowers of the field fade, and so do our adornments. Our bodies are more important than what we hang on them, and our lives are more important still. Jesus' argument is incontestable: since God gives and sustains our very lives, it follows that he will ensure transient needs like food and clothing.

CAREFREE BUT CARING DISCIPLES (MATTHEW 6:31–33)

> "So don't worry and don't keep saying, 'What shall we eat, what shall we drink, or what shall we wear?' That is what pagans are always looking for; your Heavenly Father knows that you need them all. Set your heart first on his kingdom and his goodness, and all these things will come to you as a matter of course."

It has been many years since I lost faith in Santa Claus, the Easter bunny, and the tooth fairy. They existed in my childhood because my parents provided all my physical needs and played those roles. As an adult I retain my faith in God, but not because he provides my needs in the same direct way as my parents did. Rather, as an adult, I need to cooperate and collaborate with him and with others. Writing to the Thessalonians, Paul insisted that Christians work for their needs:

> We did not eat anyone's food without paying for it. In fact we toiled and labored night and day to avoid being the slightest expense to you. This was not because we had no right to ask our necessities of you, but because we wanted to set you an example to imitate. When we were actually with you we gave you this principle to work on: "If a man will not work, he shall not eat" (2 Thessalonians 3:8–10).

We cannot expect to be fed miraculously, as the Israelites were, with manna in the desert. The birds of the air are fed not directly from God's hand but through nature. So, too, flowers grow because they take nourishment from the soil. God provides, but indirectly through nature and through *others*.

Jesus put himself in place of the needy when he said, "I was hungry and you gave me nothing to eat. I was thirsty and you gave me nothing to drink. I was a stranger and you never made me welcome. When I was naked you did nothing to clothe me; when I was sick and in prison you never cared to visit me" (Matthew 25:42–43).

His lesson: "Whatever you failed to do to the humblest of my brothers you failed to do to me" (v. 45).

THE PERSISTENCE OF PROBLEMS (MATTHEW 6:34)

> "Don't worry at all then about tomorrow. Tomorrow can worry about itself. One day's trouble is enough for one day."

Jesus is clear: despite God's providence, there will be troubles. It is worry he warns against. And nothing could be more realistic: if we are anxious about tomorrow we cannot pay attention to today and the problems and satisfactions which present themselves now. It is not only perverse but impractical for people to burden themselves with regret for the past and anxiety about the future. We live in present time alone. The time to follow Jesus is now.

What Jesus promises is that nothing will befall us without God's knowledge. To have it otherwise would be to deny human freedom to fail and require his miraculous intervention at every moment. Instead, nature will be true to itself: fire will not only warm but burn, water will not only nourish but drown, wind will not only refresh but sometimes wreak destruction. People will continue to cause harm to themselves and act perversely with one another. We are no longer the innocents our first parents were before they chose themselves over God, and the world that humankind has fashioned is no longer the original Eden.

I always find it helpful to remember this fact: there were lilies in the fields and birds in the air around Golgotha on the day Jesus, from the depths of agony on his cross, "gave a great cry and said, 'Father, I commend my spirit into your hands'" (Luke 23:46). To be sure, God's providence extends over life's tragedies as well as its blessings.

Just as it is pointless to worry about the inevitable, it is madness to be anxious about things that may never happen. People shorten their lives by worrying about developing cancer, suffering bankruptcy, or being afflicted with a myriad of mishaps. Psychoanalysts' couches are occupied by men and women who are healthy and prosperous today but are paralyzed by dread for tomorrow. Better to rest our faith in a God of abundant goodness.

As John Stott suggests, anxiety is aggravated by ambition. We fear the loss not of the things we *need* but the things we *desire*. "That is what pagans are always looking for," Jesus laments (Matthew 6:32). To follow him, we must be ambitious for God's kingdom and his righteousness. We must commit ourselves to exemplifying the good news of the gospel and God's righteousness by becoming agents of his providence this side of eternity. Because we are forgiven, and blessed, and hopeful, we have the responsibility to extend forgiveness, blessings, and hope to all of God's people.

Questions to Ponder

1. What is the purpose of fasting for a Christian?

2. What dangers are associated with self-inflicted penances?

3. How does fasting complement prayer?

4. Does God's promise of reward make our discipleship selfish?

5. Bonhoeffer warned that we must not allow even religion or personal piety to come between Christ and ourselves. How could that possibly happen?

Following in Jesus' Steps

1. *Our treasure and our heart.* What are the advantages of choosing God's treasures over my own desires?

2. *Clear-sightedness.* What does it mean for me personally to "walk in the light"?

3. *Integrity.* Can I be true to God and true to myself at the same time?

4. *Mammon.* Why is mammon an unsatisfactory alternative to God?

5. *Comedy or tragedy.* Explain which word best describes for me the life of Jesus?

The Big Question

What must I do to be the agent of God's providence?

FIVE

"DO NOT JUDGE . . ."

JUDGING OTHERS
(MATTHEW 7:1–29)

If you are taking a close look at the Sermon on the Mount for the first time, you may chuckle at Jesus' imagery. Don't be concerned; you're not being irreverent. I wouldn't be surprised if the multitudes who heard his sermon were reduced to laughter by much of what Jesus said. Can't you just hear the snickers and sighs of amusement coming from a crowd that is expected to welcome Jesus' commands as "good news"? But Jesus also knew how to use humor to drive home a point.

THE MEASURE YOU RECEIVE (MATTHEW 7:1–5)

"Don't criticize people, and you will not be criticized. For you will be judged by the way you criticize others, and the measure you give will be the measure you receive. Why do you look at the speck of sawdust in your brother's eye and fail to notice the plank in your own? How can you say to your brother, 'Let me get the speck out of your eye' when there is a plank in your own? You hypocrite! Take the plank out of your own eye first, and then you can see clearly enough to remove your brother's speck of dust."

This teaching is one more instance of Jesus' use of exaggeration to make a moral point. Earlier in the sermon, Jesus advised those in his audience who had a wandering eye to "pluck it out and throw it away" (Matthew 5:29). The venerable English critic Godfrey Smith rightly credits Jesus with "a colossal sense of humor: you care about the speck in the other chap's eye, but don't care about the beam in yours. It's hyperbole, the stock-in-trade of Jewish comedians through the ages." Without his deft use of imagery and talent for storytelling, Jesus could not have held the attention of audiences for hours at a time. Clearly, the Sermon on the Mount is not a dry treatise on ethics. Rather, it is a vivid lesson about life, filled with surprises and a sharp appreciation of human foible.

Those who aspire to follow Jesus must develop the ability to laugh at themselves. Lighthearted self-criticism is the manifestation of humility, which in turn is the honest recognition of the truth about ourselves. Did people in Jesus' audience wince when he called them hypocrites for being critical of others while approving of themselves? Probably. But is not that very discrepancy the basis of the human comedy? We must first learn to laugh at ourselves before we can accept the grace to change our ways.

As a journalist, I confess that one of my profession's conceits is objectivity, which in practice means standing aloof from people to catch them making fools of themselves. Some reporters I know have honed the art of "gotcha" journalism, deliberately luring newsmakers into traps. At the same time, journalists resist any and all attempts to reveal their own prejudices and inconsistencies. "This story is about you," they protest to those they interview, "it's not about me." This is the very attitude that Jesus condemns.

He does not expect us to turn a blind eye to the faults of others, however, even as we acknowledge our own. The truth about all of us must be acknowledged: evil as well as good, lies as well as truth, the intolerable as well as the tolerable. We would be denying our critical faculties if we failed to make value judgments. But what Jesus condemns is *censoriousness* or deliberate faultfinding. To judge people harshly is to assume the role of censor, claiming the competence and authority to lord it over others. That is not the role or the responsibility of a disciple of Jesus.

In journalism, science, and scholarship, the spirit of detachment is clearly a virtue. But in human interaction, it is often a vice. The journalist who merely stands by and reports on a tragedy without lifting a finger to help lacks a sense of proportion and compassion. The same is true for those of us who profess to be Christian. As Bonhoeffer notes:

> If we love, we can never observe the other person with detachment, for he is always and at every moment a living claim to our love and service . . . Judging others makes us blind, whereas love is illuminating.

There is but one judge—God—and we are all under his judgment. As Paul notes, "If we were closely to examine ourselves beforehand, we should avoid the judgment of God" (1 Corinthians 11:31). In that event, John Stott notes, "we would not only escape the judgment of God; we would also be in a position humbly and gently to help an erring brother."

THE PERILS OF PROSELYTISM (MATTHEW 7:6)

> "You must not give holy things to dogs, nor must you throw your pearls before pigs—or they may trample them underfoot and turn and attack you."

A seminarian, citing this passage, recently submitted an essay in class arguing that Jesus was "anti-animal." I believe the Good Shepherd and the Lamb of God would challenge this student's exegesis.

In fact, the passage has been widely misinterpreted. Augustine believed that it instructs the faithful not to reveal elements of the faith to those who are likely to reject them. A few modern scholars suggest that it means not to take the gospel to the Gentiles. More likely, as Dale C. Allison suggests, the message is that when "it is sometimes necessary to deal with the faults of others . . . one must not be meekly charitable against all reason." Bonhoeffer, following Luther, suggests this reading:

> Every attempt to impose the gospel by force, to run after people and proselytize them, to use our own resources to arrange the salvation of other people, is both futile and dangerous. It is futile, because the swine do not recognize the pearls that are cast before them, and dangerous, because it profanes the word of forgiveness, by causing those we fain would serve to sin against that which is holy. Worse still, we shall only meet with the blind rage of hardened and darkened hearts.

Jesus instructs his disciples to carry the good news of the gospel but to expect rejection:

> "If no one will welcome you or even listen to what you have to say, leave that house or town, and once outside shake off the dust of that place from your feet. . . . When they persecute you in one town make your escape to the next" (Matthew 10:14, 23).

The gospel is not an ideology, like communism, fascism, or nationalism, whose followers can become fanatical and demanding, forcing their beliefs on others. Rather, the gospel is a gift to be accepted or refused freely. No one, including Jesus himself, can force anyone to believe. To be sure, in past centuries Christian zealots forcibly baptized unbelievers, but too often they failed to make them believe. "To try and force the Word on the world by hook and by crook," Bonhoeffer says, "is to make the living Word of God into a mere idea."

Effective discipleship delivers the good news of the gospel by example, not by argument.

ASKING, SEARCHING, KNOCKING (MATTHEW 7:7–11)

> "Ask and it will be given to you. Search and you will find. Knock and the door will be opened to you. The one who asks will always receive; the one who

is searching will always find, and the door is opened to the man who knocks. If any of you were asked by his son for bread, would you give him a stone, or if he asks for a fish would you give him a snake? If you then, for all your evil, quite naturally give good things to your children, how much more likely is it that your Heavenly Father will give good things to those who ask him?"

In my book, *Be Strong and Courageous* (Sheed & Ward, 2000), I recounted the true story of the young St. Francis being cast in prison by his father. The son's crime? Selling some of his merchant father's cloth to help restore a chapel in Assisi. On his release, Francis set about rebuilding the shrine with his own hands, successfully begging stones from the townspeople for that purpose. Had Francis asked his father for bread, it's unlikely that Francis could have counted on even the gift of a stone from his hard-hearted parent!

And many of us have known of instances today when parents have not, in fact, been generous and supportive of their children. But Jesus' Father is generous to everyone who asks, searches, or knocks. At the same time, disciples have their role; they cannot expect to receive unless they are generous to others. Confidence in God is one thing; complacency, however, is something else, and it has no place in the disciple's life.

Jesus notes that parents ("for all your evil") quite naturally give good things to their children. He recognizes, too, that even self-centered adults are generous to those they love. Happily, however, God is not burdened by self-indulgence; he is love itself, so his generosity is assured and indiscriminate. Jesus identifies his Father as *our* Father, and thus emphasizes an utterly revolutionary way of conceiving God's relationship to us and our relationship to him—like parent and child, but so much more.

When, in my late teens, I began being racked with doubt, I devoted more than a decade to retrieving my religious faith. I broke an engagement to be married, briefly entered a monastery, then a seminary for years, and read philosophy and theology (as if I could find God in a book).

Finally I prayed. At length I realized that God was proving himself to me within my desperate search for him. Ultimately, unable to prove his existence by my wits, I was humbled to allow him to prove himself to me by my need for him.

Our asking, searching, and knocking are evidence that there is a God who answers. We seek the Good Shepherd in confidence because he has already made the effort to find us.

Asking, searching, and knocking, however, constitute only one kind of prayer—the kind that expresses need. And indeed, it is not selfish to ask for what we require, for ourselves and others. After praising God, seeking forgiveness, and expressing gratitude to him in prayer, we must still acknowledge our needs, which exceed knowing just where our "daily bread" is coming from.

But why is it necessary to pray at all, when Jesus assures us that God is already aware of our needs? Human parents, after all, don't wait until their children ask before feeding and clothing them. The issue, John Stott says, is not whether God is ready to give to us "but whether we are ready to receive." Whereas many parents spoil their children, God is not so inclined. Instead, he waits until we realize the extent of our need and turn to him in humility. This is not to say that God helps only those go-getters who help themselves, but rather that he wants us to be conscious of our need. Just as faith is not cocksure, Christian hope is not complacent. The apostle James reviles those who complain that their prayers are not answered:

> You crave for something and don't get it; you are murderously jealous of what you can't possess yourselves; you struggle and fight with one another. You don't get what you want because you don't ask God for it. And when you do ask he doesn't give it to you, for you ask in quite the   wrong spirit—you only want to satisfy your desires (James 4:2–3).

Jesus affirms that God "makes his sun rise upon evil men as well as good, and he sends his rain upon honest and dishonest men alike" (Matthew 5:45). If God is so evenhanded, providing for the good and the wicked alike, why should good people bother to pray? After all, God provides blessings indiscriminately (including life itself) to people whether or not they resort to prayer. Most people get their daily bread from the supermarket, by paying for it, not by praying for it. In truth, we pray to acknowledge our needs and our dependence on God.

There are gifts that come only through prayer: faith itself, forgiveness, deliverance, love, peace, and intimacy with God. These are spiritual, not natural, gifts. They can be rejected, or we can be indifferent to them. These are the very needs that the follower of Christ can pray for with confidence.

Jesus' promise that our prayers will be answered does not ensure that we will get what we want with no strings attached. After all, we are not magicians manipulating God. Our ability even to know what is good for us is limited, so we do better to rely on God's wisdom about us. In his *Studies in the Epistle of James* (New Mildmay Press, 1968), Alec Moyter confesses that if he was certain to get everything he asked for

> ... then I for one would never pray again, because I would not have sufficient confidence in my own wisdom to ask God for anything. . . . It would impose an intolerable burden on frail human wisdom if . . . God was pledged to give whatever we ask, when we ask it, and in exactly the terms we ask. How could we bear the burden?

Sages have observed that the only thing worse than failing to obtain one's heart's desire is actually getting it. Only God knows exactly what we need when we need it. But we must ask.

THE GOLDEN RULE (MATTHEW 7:12)

> "Treat other people exactly as you would like to be treated by them—this is the meaning of the Law and the Prophets."

The Golden Rule prohibits Christians from excusing faults in themselves that they castigate in others. The disciples of Jesus must recognize themselves as but one in the vast company of forgiven sinners, all of whom owe their lives to God's love. We are all equal in the sight of God, so we must deal with one another equally. Granted, Christians enjoy the advantage of the gospel, but even the good news is useless unless we discern God and serve him in others. God possesses us; we do not own him.

The key to following the Golden Rule is to imagine ourselves in the place of others: if I were that other person, how would I want to be treated? Self-absorbed and self-indulgent people will find this difficult; they are unable to get outside of their egos to act in compassionate ways. After all, the very word *compassion* implies solidarity with others. We do not just feel *for* them but are *with* them in their experience.

There is nothing novel about the Golden Rule, of course, except this: Jesus restated the common wisdom in *positive* terms. Confucius, for example wrote, "Do not do to others what you would not wish done to yourself." The same negative maxim echoes in the teachings of the Stoics. In the Old Testament Apocrypha we read, "Do not do to anyone what you yourself would hate" (Tobit 4:15). Rabbi Hillel, who may have been one of Jesus' teachers, said, "What is hateful to you, do not do to anyone else. This is the whole law; all the rest is commentary" (Talmud: Shabbath 31a).

By contrast, Jesus states the Golden Rule in positive terms: what we *must* do rather than what we must refrain from doing. And he provides justification for going out of our way to treat people fairly: the common fatherhood of God. We are all of us, in all times, places, and conditions, literally brothers and sisters—equally children of the same Father, and precious to him. We are family.

The Golden Rule not only obliges us to care for others but for ourselves as well. We are temples of God's spirit. Yet, we are as prone as unbelievers to abuse our health and shorten the lives our Creator has given us. People possess the perverse capacity to sin against themselves—from overeating to overworking, addiction, and careless health habits, literally killing themselves little by little. Indeed, a sin against oneself is a sin against the God who made us for himself. Healthy Christians, by contrast, provide for themselves and others without distinction.

Dale C. Allison observes that the Golden Rule is not a law that can be obeyed without reflection: "It is rather a general principle that requires imaginative application." So we must visualize ourselves in our neighbor's place and imagine what it is like to walk in his shoes. Then we will know how to act generously and compassionately toward him—as God does.

Note that the Golden Rule does not prescribe treating others exactly *as* they treat us. To operate on that premise would reduce human behavior to barbarism. In his sermon, Jesus has already condemned revenge and demanded that we love our enemies, returning good for evil. As Hans Küng says, "God's love of enemies is itself . . . the reason for man's love of enemies."

THE ROAD LESS TRAVELED (MATTHEW 7:13–14)

> "Go in by the narrow gate. For the wide gate has a broad road which leads to disaster and there are many people going that way. The narrow gate and the hard road lead out into life and only a few are finding it."

Bonhoeffer likens Christians to "citizens of two worlds," treading "on the razor edge between this world and the kingdom of heaven." And indeed the road is hard, the gate is narrow. Elsewhere, Jesus likens our struggles to reach the kingdom of heaven to passing through the eye of a needle. What could be more difficult for those whose entire attention is fixed on themselves?

But we are not to be discouraged. Humanly speaking, much seems impossible, but with God anything and everything is possible. Jesus' yoke is easy, his burden light (see Matthew 11:30). He is himself the narrow gate: "I am the door. If a man goes in through me, he will be safe and sound" (John 10:9).

There are but two alternatives in life—the way of the world and the way of God—and the better way is the harder of the two. Ultimately there is only *one* choice we can make if we bother to choose at all—we dare not drift, indefinitely delaying a decision. We must decide and we must make an effort. It is impossible to be a "moderate" Christian. In his autobiography, *Surprised by Joy*, C. S. Lewis reminisced about how he determined in his teens to assert his independence from authority:

> I was soon . . . altering "I believe" to "one does feel." And oh, the relief of it! . . . From the tyrannous noon of (God's) revelation I passed into the cool evening twilight of Higher Thought, where there was nothing to be obeyed, and nothing to be believed except what was either comforting or exciting.

In short, the young Lewis made up his own rules as he went along. Many years later, when he was converted to Christianity, he was forced to substitute God's revelation for his own easy inclinations. That is the hard and narrow way—and the humble way as well—because we must accept God's superior wisdom over our own.

John Stott remarks that, when following the wide road

> . . . there is evidently no limit to the luggage we can take with us. We need leave nothing behind, not even our sins, self-righteousness, or pride. The gate leading to the hard way, on the other hand, is *narrow*. One has to look for it to find it. It is easy to miss. . . . Further, in order to enter it, we must leave everything behind—sin, selfish ambition, covetousness, even if necessary family and friends. For no one can follow Christ who has not first denied himself.

Jesus remarks that only a "few are finding" the narrow road and gate. That is because few in his time were looking for it. Today it is our good fortune as Christians to know where to look.

THE GREAT DIVIDE (MATTHEW 7:15–20)

> "Be on your guard against false religious teachers, who come to you dressed up as sheep but are really

greedy wolves. You can tell them by their fruits. Do you pick a bunch of grapes from a thorn-bush or figs from a clump of thistles? Every good tree produces sound fruit, but a rotten tree produces bad fruit. A good tree cannot produce bad fruit, and a rotten tree cannot produce good fruit. The tree that fails to produce good fruit is cut down and burnt. So you may know the quality of men by what they produce."

Through the ages, Christians have been confronted with a myriad of heresies, each one an attempt to "improve" on Jesus' teaching, either by oversimplification or by dismissing things he said that are uncomfortable or inconvenient.

Ironically, the history of the Christian faith is best told by reference to teachings recognized as false. In our own time the prevalence of trendy theology forces people of faith to be alert rather than complacent.

I serve a consortium of twelve Catholic and Protestant seminaries that aim to produce ecumenically minded graduates for the priesthood and ministry. All of us are alert to the danger that, in our quest for Christian unity and interfaith understanding, we could fall prey to the complacent beliefs that there is truth in all religions and that all faiths are fundamentally the same, making the excuse that, after all, we are all responsible to the same God. To fall for such an easy faith in the quest for unity would be to deny all that Jesus came to earth to teach us and to die for.

But who are the "false religious teachers" Jesus referred to in his sermon? No one today knows for sure, but his audience at the time apparently did. Pseudo-disciples were the enemy. They patronizingly called him "Lord" and even performed wonders in his name, in hopes that some of his reputation would rub off on them. But they revealed themselves as vain and self-serving. In his letters, Paul constantly inveighs against ambitious local church leaders who presume to tamper with true religion.

Christianity is a sophisticated faith meant to be understood by simple people who worship a God who is one, yet three; who follow a Son of God who is both divine and human; who exist as creatures who are both body and soul;

and inhabit a good world in which evil flourishes. How are they to know what is true? By the character of their teachers. And how can character be discerned? By the teachers' behavior.

Jesus does not quibble about inarticulate preachers or misstated doctrine. Rather, he warns against those who, motivated by ambition, appear innocent but are "ravenous wolves." Fortunately, the greedy cannot keep up appearances for long, but will reveal themselves. In our own time, televangelists have built empires on the offerings of poor and misguided believers who seek Christ's comfort. In the process these false teachers have created their own worldly empires, opposed to the kingdom of God.

I once asked a prominent Quaker how he could be certain that the Inner Light on which he relied was telling him the truth. He replied that truth is reflected in what one *does*. One's deeds are open to view. If they are false, then they are not based on the truth, and that person is a fraud. By their fruits you shall know them.

THE TREE THAT FAILS (MATTHEW 7:15–20)

Medieval Christianity believed that false teachers, however well-intentioned, threatened the eternal salvation of the faithful. As a result, the Church sanctioned heresy hunting, because Jesus had acknowledged that trees that bear bad fruit are cut down and cast into the fire. With the perspective of history, we now realize that witch hunts were typically carried out for political reasons, not to protect religious orthodoxy. Joan of Arc was accused of heresy, then later was declared a saint.

Jesus is careful to confine his warnings to those teachers who are wolves in sheep's clothing. Sheep are helpless to defend themselves against wolves. The Good Shepherd protects his sheep, whereas the hireling abandons them to predators. Paul warned the elders at Ephesus:

> "I know that after my departure savage wolves will come in among you without mercy for the flock. Yes, and even from among you men will arise speaking perversions of the truth, trying to draw

away the disciples and make them followers of themselves. This is why I tell you to keep on the alert . . ." (Acts 20:29–31).

What are these "perversions of the truth?" The Old Testament is instructive. There the false prophets preached an easy religion—a God who was all mercy and love but never judged. Jeremiah said of them:

> They fill you with false hopes . . . They keep saying to those who despise me, "The Lord says you will have peace," and to all who follow the stubbornness of their hearts they say, "no harm will come to you" (Jeremiah 23:16–17).

False teachers preach easy optimism—what Bonhoeffer calls "cheap grace" as opposed to the "costly grace" of the gospel. It is faith without hard edges, sentiment without testing, comfort without challenge.

> "They dress the wound of my people as though it were not serious.
> 'Peace, peace,' they say, when there is no peace" (Jeremiah 8:11).

The Secret of the Sermon (Matthew 7:21–23)

> "It is not everyone who keeps saying to me 'Lord, Lord' who will enter the kingdom of Heaven, but the man who actually does my Heavenly Father's will. In 'that day' many will say to me, 'Lord, Lord, didn't we preach in your name, and do many great things in your name?' Then I shall tell them plainly, 'I have never known you. Go away from me, you have worked on the side of evil!'"

To merely confess faith in Christ (saying "Lord, Lord") gives us no right to claim Jesus for ourselves. Nor is church membership a ticket to his favor. Those whom Jesus calls belong to him and must follow him. As Bonhoeffer notes, "The church is marked off from the world not by a special

privilege, but by the gracious election and calling of God."
We must do God's will, building our lives on the grace of
God. The Christian's privilege does not consist of
mouthing the words of faith, but of acting in good faith.
Indeed, "no one could say, 'Jesus is Lord,' except by the
Holy Spirit" (1 Corinthians 12:3). The grace of Christ is a
gift that places demands on us.

Paul's beautiful discourse on love in 1 Corinthians 13
also contains his harshest warnings about false faith. Paul
acknowledges that it is possible for one to prophesy, have
all knowledge, and even the faith to move mountains, yet
still act self-indulgently, not for love of Christ. Conceivably,
giving away one's goods and even accepting martyrdom
can be done without love, without Christ, without discipleship.

Complacent Christians are content with being their
own judges and juries. But only Jesus can forgive, and he
will judge us. The most horrible words Jesus ever uttered
were, "I have never known you." Those are words we do
not want to hear, and there is no reason for him to utter
them if we respond to his word and his call rather than to
our own inclinations.

Note that the false prophets work wonders, but they do
not feed the hungry, welcome the stranger, or visit the sick.
They favor the spectacular, not the mundane. Whereas they
want to be noticed, their lives are nothing more than counterfeit dramas. The true disciple does good that is seldom
seen or acknowledged. The only true test of faith is charity.

And, indeed, that faith will be tested. The faith that
saves is not passive but proactive. It is not just assent to a
creed or acceptance of revelation. To accept adoption as
God's sons and daughters does not permit us to act like
hapless children all our lives. We must grow up in faith,
acting on it—and that will mean, invariably, our faith will
be tested. In our roles and privileges as Jesus' followers, we
cannot be content to leave all the work to him. He has
already paid the ultimate price to redeem the world. It is
now our turn to confirm what he did.

In Luke's version of the sermon, Jesus demands, "What is the point of calling me 'Lord, Lord', without doing what I tell you to do? . . . A man's words express what overflows from his heart" (Luke 6:45–46). Rest assured, there is no contradiction between faith and "works"—the faith that saves is a working faith. Faith cannot be private; it has public responsibilities.

FOUNDATIONS ON ROCK (MATTHEW 7:24–27)

"Everyone then who hears these words of mine and puts them into practice is like a sensible man who builds his house on rock. Down came the rain and up came the floods, while the winds blew and roared upon that house—and it did not fall because its foundations were on rock. And everyone who hears these words of mine and does not follow them can be compared with a foolish man who built his house on sand. Down came the rain and up came the floods, while the winds blew and battered that house till it collapsed, and fell with a great crash."

There are many denominations within Christianity, but just one faith, one baptism, one Lord of all. Still, we can choose to rest our faith on either a firm or a shifting foundation. The house built on sand is a faith resting on sentiment—a passive, complacent faith that takes comfort from and delight in Jesus, relies on him, but turns a deaf ear to his demand that we follow him. This kind of faith cannot survive life's tempests. As reformer John Calvin warned, "True piety is not fully distinguished from its counterfeit till it comes to the trial."

Faith's only firm foundation is Jesus' Sermon on the Mount. Those who build a life of faith and action on the sermon and on following him will not only survive life's trial, but prevail over them. We are called to imitate Christ, wherever he leads.

Questions to Ponder

1. Why does Jesus exaggerate to make a moral point?

2. Why is a sense of humor and the ability to laugh at oneself indispensable to every Christian?

3. Why is the good news of the gospel more effectively spread by example than by argument?

4. What does Bonhoeffer mean when he says that "we can only seek God when we know him already"?

5. "The only thing worse than failing to obtain our heart's desire is to get it." Explain this irony. Give examples.

Following in Jesus' Steps

1. *The Golden Rule.* What do I do specifically to follow the Golden Rule.

2. *Prayer.* God seems to reward people who never pray. So why should I pray?

3. *Faith versus action.* Since we are justified by faith, why can't I be content with just believing?

4. *False prophets.* What are the messages of the false prophets I hear and why do I find their messages appealing?

5. *Judgment.* What might I do to merit Jesus saying "I have never known you"?

The Big Question

How can I admit to my own faults without being discouraged, and acknowledge the faults of others without feeling superior?

PART TWO

THE
COMMITMENT

SIX

THE WILL AND
THE WAY

The Sermon on the Mount is neither a buffet nor an à la carte menu. The disciple cannot pick and choose what to put on his plate, rejecting some entrees as indigestible or too salty or too sweet. The sermon is what Jesus lays before us. If we reject it, we will starve.

"Humanly speaking," Bonhoeffer admits, "we could understand and interpret the Sermon on the Mount in a thousand different ways. Jesus knows only one possibility: simple surrender and obedience, not interpreting it or applying it, but doing and obeying it." He adds: "It is impossible to want to do it and yet not do it." So if we can summon the will, God will provide the grace for us to follow in Jesus' steps. As Paul acknowledged, "I am ready for anything through the strength of the One who lives within me" (Philippians 4:13).

The multitudes were astonished at Jesus' words, because they recognized that the Son of God had the power to pass judgment on the world and to demand that humankind follow him. To those who agreed to follow, he offered hope. His message: forget fate, trust providence. Life is neither tragic nor brief. It is an eternal reward for those who love God and honor his will in their lives.

But does the disciple follow Jesus only for a reward? Is the imitation of Christ prompted by selfish motive? No, not at all. We belong to God. He calls us to himself for himself.

As Augustine acknowledged, our restless hearts will not be satisfied until they rest in him. God's kingdom is not a reward, because we do not merit God's promise. Rather, it is our destiny which, while not earned, can yet be lost if we thwart God's graciousness. When God created us as free creatures, the terrible possibility arose that we could choose ourselves and ignore him. To follow Christ is to choose God over ourselves and vindicate his love for us.

CONFIDENT CHRISTIANITY

People who lack faith may admire the Sermon on the Mount as an ideal, but it takes faith in Jesus' authority to accept the sermon as a standard of living. Motivation to embrace that standard rests on faith that Christ is more than a moral teacher. He is the Son of God, who offers certain hope of eternal life.

Even a cursory reading of the Gospels reveals a Jesus of quiet confidence, not a flamboyant preacher who impressed by histrionics. He spoke calmly but never minced his words. He neither cajoled nor threatened. Although he references his teaching by recalling the ancient Scriptures, he did not base his authority on Moses and the patriarchs. His teaching was not circumscribed by his upbringing as a faithful Jew. Rather, he spoke directly for God, claiming him as his Father, and he taught in universal terms relevant to everyone regardless of nationality and culture. Jesus possessed the key to God's kingdom and could open it to everyone.

One of the striking characteristics of Jesus' authority was its personal nature. Again and again in the sermon Jesus said, "Truly, truly *I* say to you," even daring to contradict the corruptions of Moses' teaching: "But *I* say to you . . ." He spoke with utter confidence because he was on intimate terms with the Source of his teachings: "My teaching is not really mine but comes from the One who sent me" (John 7:16).

Our human relationships can help us better understand faith *in* Jesus, which every disciple must have. If I ask a stranger what time it is, I have no reason not to believe that person's answer. All I am doing is trusting a fact. And even if that stranger, for whatever reason, gives me the wrong information, the consequences to our "relationship" are minimal; we *don't have* a relationship. There is little need for me to have confidence *in* that person.

But in my marriage I believe in a person. That means trust, confidence, and love in another human being. I am faithful to my marriage because I have faith *in* my wife and her fidelity to me. I don't expect her to be knowledgeable about everything (although she's mighty smart!), but I believe in her. That is the kind of faith one needs to confidently follow Jesus.

But where can you find such confidence? Some scholars approach the Gospels with skepticism because they do not reveal all we might like to know about the "historical" Jesus. But today's disciples understand that the Gospels were written as testimonies of faith, that they reveal the Jesus whom the first disciples believed *in*: the Jesus of faith. There is no reason to doubt that the Jesus who was loved and trusted by his friends and disciples was the same Jesus his enemies arrested and crucified. If Judas or Pilate or the Pharisees had left us an account of Jesus' life, you can be sure that it would not read like the testimonies of Matthew, Mark, Luke, or John, because his enemies did not believe in him.

Meet Jesus in the Gospels. He compels your confidence. Meet him as well in the letters of St. Paul—the most poignant "sermons" ever preached. Meet him in your prayers and find the confidence to follow him.

FAITH AS A HABIT

Faith is a *habit*. Confidence comes from *habitual* faith. Anyone who is good at anything derives his or her confidence from training and experience. In the same manner, Christians gain confidence and motivation by "putting on the mind of Christ"—breaking through their egos to see themselves from God's point of view—*habitually*. In other words, the confident Christian views life by the light of faith. When G. K. Chesterton sought vacation lodgings by the sea, he did not inquire of the landlady how often she changed the guests' bed linens or what she served for breakfast. That, he allowed, would be impolitic. Rather, he asked her: "What is your theology of the universe?" Chesterton's point? If the landlady possessed the faith that she lived in an orderly universe watched over by a responsible God who loved her and offered her hope, then she would likely be generous with clean sheets and hearty breakfasts for her guests! The habits of her life would reflect the habit of her faith.

"Do whatever he tells you," Jesus' mother told the servants on the occasion of his first miracle (John 2:4). That is precisely what all disciples do; because their faith is a habit of trusting in Jesus, they invite others to do the same. For nominal Christians, to contemplate following the Sermon on the Mount seems extraordinary. But among those for whom faith is a habit, I suspect we would be astounded to find many men and women who actually do imitate Christ. We are unaware of their numbers because Jesus was no show-off, nor are his followers. They intend their following of Christ to be *ordinary*.

Of course, Christian confidence can be shaken if it is not rooted in the love of God. I am often asked by Christians how they can console friends and loved ones who are in pain or have suffered loss. I answer that Christianity is not an especially consoling faith. A religion that required God's Son to die in agony on a cross is not a comforting faith, but its harshness is true to our experience of life's realities. And it portrays a self-sacrificing God of love who is worthy of our faith.

FAITH AS A KITE STRING

The English are arguably the most civilized people on earth, which may explain why my wife and I are unrepentant Anglophiles. But they are also among the least religious people on earth. Fewer than a million Englishmen and Englishwomen worship regularly in that nation's established church.

A. A. Gill of London's *Sunday Times* is Britain's most celebrated columnist. He is a maverick, who writes sexy novels in his spare time, cohabits with a woman known to the nation only as "The Blonde," struggles as a recovered alcoholic and drug addict, and literally dragged himself out of the gutter to sobriety. He also happens to be a confirmed Christian, which befuddles and occasionally scandalizes his readers.

Gill typically confines himself to writing about food and television, but not long ago another newspaper prompted him to reveal his religious faith. Here is his account of the interview:

> "A Christian!" my interviewer gasped. "A Christian as in believing in God, the God, that God?"
>
> Oh dear. Yes, that God.
>
> "You're not, you can't possibly be." (Now, remember, she'd just found out that I'd been a drug dealer, spent adult years wetting beds, smoking cigarettes out of the gutter, sleeping in dog baskets, drinking vodka through a straw for breakfast, and seeing spiders the size of human heads, all of which had elicited no more than an encouraging ho-hum.)
>
> Well, there it is. I'm outed as a Christian, proud to be godly. The problem with faith, though, is that you can't just dump it (like clothes that have gone out of fashion). Faith can leave you, you can't leave it. And try as I might to pretend I haven't caught it, I'm stuck with it . . .
>
> Atheists always [pretend to] know more about what I believe than I do. They say you believe in the resurrection and hell and plagues of frogs. Well, no and yes, I don't know. The thing about faith is that it isn't a fact—if it were provable, it wouldn't be faith. So we [Christians] never win the argument, because God isn't in the argument, he's in the absence of argument, in the space between words.
>
> Believing in God is like holding up one end of a string that disappears up into the clouds and occasionally tugs. Now I can say there's a kite at the end and somebody else may say it's a balloon. We can't possibly know, all I know is that I'm holding this string—oh, and by the way, it's invisible string.
>
> What annoys me is when agnostics tell me that my faith is based on superstition and fear, a fear of

death, fear of responsibility, that it's an easy option. You think this is easy? You think that the weight of all that paternal expectation is easy? And you imagine that knowing there might be a reckoning in the end makes morality easy? Get a life. Get a faith! It's [thinking] that ultimately you're your own policeman and judge and jury that's easy, and I wish I could do it. (I can't).

A journalist once asked Einstein if he still believed in miracles. Tell me what isn't a miracle, he replied, and that's it. Either everything is a miracle or nothing is, and most of those who believe the former are getting fewer . . . But Christianity started with 11 members and was at its strongest and purest. If it goes back to being 11, or if I'm the only poor [believer] left afflicted with it, it will make no difference. God will still be there and will still love us unrequited. The world was still round when nobody believed it.

Actually, science has the best explanation of faith, and I make no apology for [borrowing] one of its ideas. You cannot see a black hole in space, they were discovered by noticing how other stars were moved by an irresistible invisible force. That's how it is with faith.

Gill challenges his readers: "If you think that's just more of the same nebulous, sentimental, intellectually bereft old hogwash, then tough, I'm not arguing on your terms anymore."

WHEN FAITH FALTERS

Those who lack faith claim that they either have sought it in vain or they are doing very well without God, thank you. The premise—the utterly erroneous assumption— underlying both positions is that faith is something people must seek or contrive.

People do not need to seek God but only acknowledge that he has already found them. In Francis Thompson's celebrated poem, "The Hound of Heaven," God relentlessly pursues his creatures through life's labyrinth to love and save them. And in Scripture, Jesus styled himself as the Good Shepherd who expects his sheep to lose their way, and pursues the sheep until he finds them. Christians believe ourselves to be foundlings who have been found. All that is required of us is to accept the fact and follow our Shepherd.

If we are faithful, hopeful, and loving in life, we will also be confident. The following of Christ requires faith, but it delivers the confidence we need to keep us motivated. The truth of our faith is not a function of intelligence, but of fidelity—God's faith in us, and our faith in him. As Christians, we are blessed with the ability to view faith from the *inside*, because we have met Jesus—an advantage missing to Christianity's critics. Others may demand of us, "How can you believe these things?" Our answer is, "There is nothing better to be believed. To believe nothing is to live without hope. A faithful God is worthy of our faith."

Sharing Your Faith

Confidence is not a weapon to wield against the faithless. I have encountered Christian apologists who marshal logic and Scripture in an attempt to vanquish skeptics. Their erudition can be occasionally devastating, but it is ultimately impotent. No one can be beaten into submitting to faith, and confidence is not certainty. Faith cannot be imposed, only graciously accepted. That is why confident Christians who emulate Christ exercise humility and courtesy, sharing their faith by personal example. When we encounter a person with deep and loving faith and who lives a life of service—as Jesus did—we want to be like that person.

The first believers embraced faith in the risen Jesus not because it was persuasive, but because it was a gift—a surprise no one had predicted or even imagined until it happened. Our faith has never lost that compelling attraction, which is personified in Jesus and, by extension, in those who follow his example. By definition, the gospel is good news that will be as good today and tomorrow as it was two thousand years ago. As a journalist, I am humbled by the knowledge that yesterday's newspaper is good only for wrapping cold ashes from the fireplace to pitch into the trash. But the good news that undergirds our faith will always be fresh. You and I will grow old, but our God and his gospel will always be young. It will never face retirement.

People became Christians and become Christians today because they wanted and needed what they saw Christians doing, which explains why the earliest believers were willing to die for their faith. For them, faith was life itself. Their fervor is difficult to find or even appreciate today, when religious faith is routinely treated as an option—something to take or leave depending on whether one is inclined to be "religious" or not.

Faith today is, for many Christians, only a part-time occupation—an activity for a few hours on Sunday. Ironically, we have reached this casual stage because our secular culture has absorbed Christian values without acknowledging their origin in faith and in the person of Jesus. What the disciple must do is acknowledge that the best of our values come from Christ. They are what God means us to adhere to.

THE DISCIPLE AS PROPHET

I am often privileged to speak to aspiring Christian writers, encouraging their work. I assure them that they are in the business of revelation. Just like the prophets of old, writers today get rejected again and again. The Israelites didn't want to buy Isaiah's or Jeremiah's stories either. And although those prophets didn't receive the standard rejection letters writers do today ("Sorry, your submission doesn't suit our needs"), they were rejected all the same. Still, they kept communicating despite the criticism. The prophets told their audience what they didn't necessarily want to hear: that a faithful God demands fidelity in return. In short, they told them of wonderful things that required effort to make happen.

Like Christian writers, those of us who seek to follow Jesus are in the truth-telling business. To be sure, the truth makes people free, but many people (like the grumbling Israelites wandering in the Sinai) find bondage more comfortable. The Hebrew prophets were men and women, rich and poor, eccentric and scholarly. Some used poetry, others employed drama to reveal God to his people. No matter: what they possessed in common was their consistent, unchanging dedication to express the will of their God.

Isaiah, who lived all his life in Jerusalem in the eighth century before Christ, typifies the prophets (Isaiah 61). At the age of twenty-five he had a vision that God sought a prophet willing to speak God's word. Isaiah immediately answered, "Here I am. Send *me*!"

Isaiah wrote at a time of social and spiritual upheaval. He didn't stop with inspiring his readers. Instead he wrote about politics, military matters, social justice, and idolatry. Today, twenty-eight centuries later, I receive a lot of hate mail from readers of my syndicated column, because I write about the same topics. People of faith must stand up for their beliefs without inflicting them on others. When they reflect on everyday life, religious writers are guaranteed to irritate some people. It comes with the territory; it's their job as prophets.

Jesus paid Isaiah the greatest possible compliment when, in the synagogue in Nazareth, he quoted the prophet:

> The Spirit of the Lord is upon me,
> Because he has anointed me to bring good news to
> the poor;
> He hath sent me to proclaim release to the captives,
> And recovering of sight to the blind,
> To set at liberty them that are bruised,
> To proclaim the acceptable year of the Lord.
> (Isaiah 61:1; Luke 4:18–19)

Jesus let others tell his story. To our knowledge, the only words he wrote himself were figures he drew in the dirt—which no one read. He taught principally by example; his disciples do the same to this day.

TEACHING BY EXAMPLE

Whoever undertakes to follow Christ will do it humbly, sincerely, mercifully, and sometimes sorrowfully—always seeking justice and peace, forgiving those who oppose them, claiming no special privilege for themselves. These are the attitudes common to all disciples, sanctioned by Jesus himself in the Beatitudes. And this is the essence of teaching by example.

But each man and woman will follow him in ways that match their temperament and intelligence, not to mention their time, place, and culture. Consider the saints. Unlike the common run of humankind, they are not noted for their sameness, but are remarkable for their variety and uniqueness. While emulating Christ, they do not conform to a single pattern. All follow the unique paths of their own lives, each at his or her own pace and gait.

All disciples possess the same motivation (to seek God's kingdom and cherish the pearl of great price), the same mission (to do God's will and serve others), and the same virtue (love). But because they must make decisions in real-life situations, they may differ in their grasp of God's will.

Committed Christians today, for example, honestly disagree on issues of life and death, uncertain what Jesus would do. All revere life, of course, but some would put the life of the mother before that of her unborn child. Some believe that contraception itself thwarts God's power to give life. Others believe that Christian mercy demands giving terminally ill patients in agony the option of ending their lives.

In the absence of consensus, these moral issues have such widespread consequences that government is pressed to set standards for what is legally permissible, short of what is ethically ideal. Committed Christians all agree that revenge is wrong and that violence is evil, yet they disagree on whether government, in their name, may take the lives of criminals or employ violence to protect the citizenry against threat of violence.

Those who seek to follow Christ also disagree on issues of homosexuality: whether to bless gay couples or even accept active homosexuals into Christian fellowship. How can Christians determine what Jesus would do—and thus what they are to do—when confronted by such challenges?

In humility, all disciples must admit that they know only what their master did, not what he would do. Jesus simply did not address certain moral issues in his own time. If he had expressed himself clearly on the issue of slavery, for example, its practice might not have persisted in Christian countries for nearly nineteen centuries. But it was Jesus' mission to redeem us, not to solve our social problems. He left their resolution to us.

What Jesus did make clear is the spirit in which his followers must act when we are conflicted. We must be slow to anger and judgment: "Let the one among you who has never sinned throw the first stone . . . " (John 8:7).

The Sermon on the Mount reveals Jesus to be the sublime teacher, but it was easy for his enemies then and now to dismiss what he had to say as mere words. What was unique about Jesus is that he exemplified in action what he preached. He was true to his word. He not only preached the good news but lived it and died for it. Occasionally, preaching can be persuasive; example, however, is always persuasive. If we will imitate Christ, we will not only *be* good but *do* good. The needy will notice, and the world will be better for our following him.

IMITATING CHRIST

Thomas á Kempis, the author of *The Imitation of Christ*, entered a monastery at the age of twenty. There he led a serene and uneventful life until 1471, when he died at the age of ninety-one. He was remembered by his contemporaries as a shy, genial man who liked "books and quiet corners all his days."

Not surprisingly, his formula for emulating Jesus is more suitable for a solitary monk than for an active Christian with a job and family responsibilities. *The Imitation*'s chapter titles offer a taste of the kind of life Thomas advocated:

- Contempt of All of the Vanities of the World

- Humble Conceit of Ourselves

- Inordinate Affections

- Vain Hope and Pride

- Shun Familiarity

- Obedience and Subjection

- Avoid Superfluity of Words

- Profit of Adversity

- Human Misery

- Meditation on Death

- Avoid Curious Inquiries

- Self-denial

- Unworthy of Comfort, Deserving of Stripes.

The monk Thomas withdrew from life to imitate Christ and to devote his days to purifying his spirit. In sharp contrast, the disciples who surrounded Jesus were sent by him—thrust into the world—to spread the gospel. Moreover, Jesus himself, while he frequently retreated to pray, lived a life of action, not seclusion. Thus, the practical imitation of Christ must suit the lifestyles of active men and women.

Recall that the Sermon on the Mount, although addressed to the multitudes, drew their attention to Jesus' disciples, who were already living the Beatitudes. In the master's company, they were perforce humbleminded, remorseful, poor, merciful, and sincere. They, like him, sought justice and peace. They, like him, were scorned.

But they were also *happy*, for the kingdom was theirs. They were promised courage and comfort. The whole earth would belong to them. They would be fully satisfied. Mercy would be shown to them. They would see God!

So the imitation of Christ must be upbeat: "Be glad, then, yes, be tremendously glad," Jesus encouraged his followers. He encourages us as well.

Even a cursory reading of the Gospels reveals Jesus to be anything but conventionally pious. He weeps, he laughs, he heals, he forgives, he rejoices, he encourages, he fumes with anger. He is the best of friends: the man for others. He feeds the poor, heals the sick, comforts the lonely, clothes the naked, and sows peace amid enmity. He loves indiscriminately and he gives hope.

This is the Jesus to imitate.

IMMERSED IN THE WORLD

Whoever would emulate Jesus cannot do it alone but must join with others, serving them and collaborating with them. Personal piety is tested by our loving service of others. In the waning days of the Roman Empire, pious Christians became solitaries—hermits living alone in the desert, abandoning a collapsing civilization. They became eccentrics, begging food, railing against the world, and doing no one much good.

It was the genius of early Christianity to gather the hermits into economically self-sustaining communities—the monasteries—and to impose upon them the disciplines of work, prayer, and community life. The monasteries became laboratories that tested the virtues of mutual love and service.

But you and I do not live as monks. We must emulate Christ by love and service in the world, not within monastery walls. To follow the Sermon on the Mount we must be in the world, but not *of* it. Christianity does not shrink into itself; rather, it is a missionary faith. It expands. It serves. It delivers good news.

People's real needs cannot be served by faceless government but by loving service. Contemporary disciples, working through churches and voluntary agencies, do what their master did: they assist the poor and afflicted, bringing them comfort and hope. The demands for active discipleship are great, even in affluent America.

Poverty in our nation, for example, is not confined to racial minorities in cities. The majority of poor Americans are white and live outside the cities, where we cannot see them. To be poor in spirit is a virtue; to be destitute is a vice.

Meanwhile, families are broken. Police are hard-pressed to secure the domestic peace. In intact families, both spouses must work to make their way, leaving latchkey children to fend for themselves after school. Today our public schools must restrain students before they can even hope to educate them.

The students who resist restraint go to jail. Increasingly, as a nation, we lock up our problems instead of attempting to solve them. Two million of our fellow citizens are already behind bars, populating the largest penal system of any nation in history. Nearly another three million Americans are on probation, parole, or awaiting trial. Incarceration and execution have become the solutions of choice for the nation's problems.

This, indeed, is a litany of our world's serious pain. Today's disciples of Jesus do not hide from or ignore these realities. Rather, they immerse themselves deeply into the pain—sometimes by circumstance and sometimes by choice—and bring their confident faith to the healing that is desperately needed.

Fortunately, like voices in the wilderness, Christian advocacy groups are attempting to accomplish what many churches have largely abandoned: bringing the values of the Sermon on the Mount to serve the needy. Four hundred such groups were in existence at the end of World War II. They have since been joined by some five hundred more. Many of these groups are interdenominational and self-funded, operating on a shoestring.

According to Mel Reese, the director of the Ecumenical Alliance for Peace and Justice, "The church's social role is not to design a perfect society. It's to make the existing society *more* caring. Justice means taking care of one another." There is ample evidence that Americans are failing one another in pursuing a just society for all.

Today the United States leads the developed world in divorce, single-parent families, abortion, sexually transmitted diseases, child poverty, incarceration, and executions, as well as drug use and out-of-wedlock births among teens. We deny health care to a larger percentage of citizens than any other developed nation.

Former secretary of education William J. Bennett paints a picture of an uncaring nation:

> The nation we live in today is more violent and vulgar, coarse and cynical, rude and remorseless, deviant and depressed, than the one we once inhabited. A popular culture that is often brutal, gruesome, and enamored with death robs many children of their innocence. People kill other people, and themselves, more easily. Men and women abandon each other, and their children, more readily. Marriage and the American family are weaker, more unstable.

Our world cries out for men and women who follow the Sermon on the Mount. In the next chapter we look at four who succeeded.

Questions to Ponder

1. Why can't we pick and choose among the Beatitudes?

2. Does the disciple follow Jesus only for a reward? Explain.

3. The Sermon on the Mount is universally admired but seldom embraced in practice. Why?

4. Jesus spoke with total assurance. What was the source of that confidence?

5. What is the difference between believing something and believing in someone?

Following in Jesus' Steps

1. *Confidence.* Where do I find confidence as a Christian?

2. *Faith.* How can I make faith a habit?

3. *God.* A. A. Gill says to nonbelievers: "God isn't in the argument, he's in the absence of argument, in the space between words." What does this mean to me?

4. *Belonging.* What is my strongest reason for being a Christian? What is my weakest reason?

5. *Good news.* Why did the first Christians believe the gospel? Why are Christians today so prone to doubt? Why do I believe it?

The Big Question

When I am unsure of God's will, how do I decide what to do?

SEVEN

Four Who
Followed

W e will not solve all the world's problems by following Christ. However fervent our discipleship, the world will remain a fickle, dangerous, often violent place.

Nor by emulating Jesus will we solve our own personal problems. We will still be prone to accident, illness, ill-fortune, aging, heartbreak, and the indifference and enmity of our fellow human beings that Jesus suffered. In the garden he told his disciples, "My heart is breaking with a death-like grief; stay here and keep watch with me" (Matthew 26:38).

The problem we will solve by imitating Christ is *ourselves*. From a scattered, unfocused life we will achieve singleness of heart. We will convert self-indulgence into love and service. Granted, we will not solve the world's problems or escape our own troubles, but the world will be a better place for our presence in it, and we will become the persons God intended us to be from the beginning of time. We will inherit God's kingdom this side of eternity.

Our Christian faith is best understood when we witness the behavior of those who live the gospel. To put a face on the meaning of discipleship, I have chosen four Christians to illustrate the practical imitation of Christ. Each followed him in a different way, but through love and service. These people are not canonized saints; rather, they are ordinary persons who led extraordinary lives in following Jesus.

Each of these persons remained flawed but fervent; one ended badly. Like Jesus' first followers, however, they ventured forth into the world like sheep among wolves—and they succeeded because they were as wise as serpents and harmless as doves. Perhaps something in their example will resonate with our own wish to imitate Christ.

1. MITCH SNYDER

Mitch was the least likely of saints; he was an ex-convict who ended his own life in 1990, at the age of forty-six. Years earlier, he had left a wife and two children to pursue an uncertain destiny, then failed in an attempt at reconciliation with his family. In his brief life, Mitch annoyed a nation and blackmailed a president. Yet, he exemplified the Beatitudes in his efforts to feed the poor and shelter the homeless. His ultimate weapon was abstaining from food and water to draw attention to the needy.

In 1984 Mitch went fifty-one days without food, losing sixty pounds, to get then-president Ronald Reagan to renovate a government-owned building for the homeless in Washington, D.C. When the offer was withdrawn by the president, Mitch went on two more fasts. After four days without food or water, the White House finally agreed to provide $965,000 in repairs. Congress added $4 million. The shelter housed 1,200 homeless men and women and served 800 more. Later, a sixty-three-day fast left Mitch's health so impaired that he required an operation to restore vision in one eye.

Mitch's opponents dubbed him "Hollywood Mitch" and considered him a hotheaded publicity seeker with a martyr complex. His advocates considered him a cranky saint. Jesse Jackson likened him to Gandhi and Martin Luther King, and the *Washington Post* compared him to Francis of Assisi. Martin Sheen portrayed him in a TV-movie entitled *Samaritan*.

In his twenties, Mitch was a well-paid management consultant in New York. Later he told a reporter that he awoke one night in a cold sweat and asked himself if this was all there was. Abandoning work and family, he traveled to California in a car rented with a stolen credit card, and was subsequently arrested and placed in federal prison in Danbury, Connecticut. There he met the brother-priests Daniel and Philip Berrigan, who were incarcerated for their protests for peace and social justice.

Upon his release in 1972, Mitch went to Washington, D.C. to join the Community for Creative Nonviolence, which soon switched from antiwar protests to advocacy for the homeless. For the rest of his life Mitch lived with the homeless, wore donated clothes, and slept on the streets to dramatize their plight.

"He had a way of making you feel ashamed of yourself," wrote Chuck Conconi in the *Washington Post*. Mitch's motto was that the disenfranchised "need to kick in doors when necessary." He explained that he had been "called to live a different kind of life. You don't argue with God."

Mitch was not always successful in his efforts, however. In 1976 he wrote to more than eleven hundred churches, synagogues, and mosques in the Washington area to ask if they would offer space and comfort to homeless people. Only one answered yes. Two years later, he began an extended fast to persuade a prosperous church in Georgetown to divert its construction funds to his homeless shelter. Its pastor, Fr. James English, refused, remarking, "It was like having a gun pointed at my head." But on the Sunday after Mitch's death, clergy throughout the nation's capital offered public prayers for him.

The pacifist journalist Colman McCarthy said of Mitch that "he exemplified Pascal's thought: not to be mad is a form of madness." Mitch was both mad and angry, grounded in the Gospel of St. Luke, which depicts Jesus as a dissenter and troublemaker. Still, in the1980s Snyder took tea with Barbara Bush and had dinner with Jim Wright, Speaker of the House. In the *Washington Post*, Colman McCarthy observed that Mitch

> . . . was remarkably, almost heroically, nonjudgmental toward middle- and upper-class people who wanted to help but were morally clubfooted and didn't know how. "Don't just come in from the suburbs with your Volvos packed with canned foods," he would say. "Be to the people in the shelters as you are to the comfortable and well-off in your own

neighborhoods. . . . The true succor is just to relax and be present to people, because that's what the people really need. That's the hardest thing to do.'"

After Mitch's suicide Tom Bethell, in *National Review*, expressed reluctant admiration for him:

He was using the method of modern liberalism (blaming society as a whole for the failure of individuals to take responsibility for their lives) and carrying it to uncomfortable extremes. Liberals knew they had no principle of resistance to their own principle. So they couldn't stop him if he went too far.

Friendly critics complained that Mitch oversimplified the causes of the homelessness. The Rev. John Steinbruck, a fellow advocate for the homeless in Washington, said that people were "warehoused and packed in" at Mitch's three-story, block-long shelter. "You don't mix the mentally ill with felons and drug addicts," he protested.

Mitch's father abandoned his family when Mitch was just nine. Left to fend for himself, Mitch became a delinquent and, at the age of sixteen, was arrested and sent to reform school for breaking into parking meters. He carried the scars of his father's abandonment all his life, once telling a reporter, "That wasn't a good thing to do to a kid, to leave him without a father. I grew up swearing never, ever to do to my kids what my father had done to me." Yet, that's exactly what Mitch did in 1969, after six years of marriage that produced two sons.

On a rainy July afternoon in 1990, Mitch's death was announced to crowds milling on the sidewalks near his shelter, just a few blocks from the Capitol. In *People* magazine Charles E. Cohen reported on the scene: "A woman's voice began to rise and fall, rise and fall, like the sound of an approaching siren. 'Who will take care of us now?' she keened. 'Who will take care of us now?'"

In an appreciation in *U.S. News & World Report*, David Whitman noted:

Countless Americans who are intelligent, competent, and decent will likely leave the world much the

same as when they came into it. Mitch Snyder
didn't. In so doing, he reminded us that zealotry, not
just love, makes the world go around . . .

Yet, for all his passion, Snyder will never be
remembered with the same reverence reserved for a
Nelson Mandela or a Vaclav Havel. Heroes, after all,
prosper when readily identifiable villains flourish.
Snyder's blackguards lacked the unambiguously evil
character of apartheid or a totalitarian police state.

Nearly nine years after his death, the ashes of Mitch
Snyder were scattered among the graves of homeless people outside Luther Place Memorial Church in downtown
Washington. Nearly one hundred people removed their
shoes to stand on what the church's minister called holy
ground. Carol Fennelly, Mitch's longtime companion,
placed a white rose on the ashes. "I think he left behind a
legacy of courage," she said. "In the face of everyone telling
him that his dream of a world without homelessness could
not become a reality, he persevered. That takes tremendous
courage."

Fennelly moved to Ohio, where she founded Hope
House in Youngstown to provide family services for seventeen hundred District of Columbia prisoners transferred
there. She recalls Mitch's plans to take a leave of absence
and retreat to a Trappist monastery in April 1990. "I think
he got very tired. I think I failed him in that I wasn't there
when he needed me."

The body of Mitch Snyder, saint and sinner, was found
on July 5, 1990, in the homeless shelter he managed. Not
long before his death, he had admitted, characteristically, "I
bring out a lot of good in people, but I ain't Mother Teresa."

2. ELIZABETH FRY

Elizabeth's Quaker contemporaries accused her of neglect-
ing her twelve children and of an "unladylike involvement
in worldly affairs." One wit remarked, "We long to burn
her alive." His reason? "Examples of living virtue give
birth to distressing comparison."

Throughout her life Elizabeth Fry was less concerned with her virtue than with her effectiveness in following Christ. In the Gospels Jesus issues a challenge: "When I was sick and in prison you never cared to visit me" (Matthew 25:43), lamenting that "whatever you failed to do to the humblest of my brothers you failed to do to me" (v. 45). Elizabeth not only responded to Jesus' challenge but thoroughly reformed and humanized the treatment of prisoners.

Like most saints, Elizabeth had her flaws—in her case, a predilection for port, ale, and laudanum; a relish for public admiration; and a delight in the company of the rich and celebrated. She could at times be proud, ruthless, and selfish, but always in the pursuit of good. But Elizabeth battled her own demons; her mother died when Elizabeth was only thirteen and, for the rest of her life, Elizabeth was prone to suicidal depression.

Elizabeth Gurney Fry was born into a large and prosperous Quaker family in Norwich, England, in 1780. Although she pursued her mission until her death at the age of sixty-five, she did not really find it until she was thirty-six. A slow student, she was often called "stupid" by her sisters. From the age of six she suffered anxiety attacks and nightmares, and was terrified of the dark.

Just before Elizabeth's seventeenth birthday, her family hosted Prince William Frederick, nephew of King George III, at Earlham, their country home. Later the prince would champion Elizabeth's work for prison reform. Also at the age of seventeen, Elizabeth encountered an American Quaker minister, William Savery, whose example and preaching transformed her life.

At eighteen, Elizabeth started a school for the children of weavers, and taught poor adults to read and write. She fed and clothed the poor in the neighborhood and tended to the sick, reading the Bible aloud in a "melodious" voice that would serve her well during her prison ministry. A female Quaker minister, Deborah Darby, prophesied that the adolescent Elizabeth would become "a light to the blind, speech to the dumb, and feet to the lame."

Increasingly embarrassed by her pampered upbringing, Elizabeth began to discipline herself, rising early, dressing plainly, and boldly confronting her anxieties. On trips to London, she made a point of walking at night down dangerous streets. At nineteen, she overcame her fear of speaking in public by giving testimony at her Meeting, although she admitted she "shook from head to foot."

Before she turned twenty, Elizabeth married Joseph Fry, a plain-living Quaker from a wealthy tea-importing family. Some characterized Fry as a long-suffering spouse dominated by his wife, but it was a happy marriage, and Joseph's willingness to manage the Fry household in Elizabeth's absence enabled her to carry out her ministry, even as she bore twelve sons and daughters, the last when she was forty-two.

By the time she was twenty-four and the mother of three children under the age of five, Elizabeth began prowling the streets of London at night, feeding and clothing destitute women and their children. By day she brought comfort, provisions, and the gospel to the city's poor in workhouses, and invited them for hot meals in her own home.

Despite Elizabeth's efforts, however, poverty increased, primarily due to cultural and political events of the time. The Industrial Revolution was replacing workers with machines, expanding unemployment. Strapped for cash because of the Napoleonic Wars, the government turned its back on those most in need of its assistance. Finally, a poor harvest in 1812 caused food shortages so great that Samuel Johnson calculated that a thousand men, women, and children were starving to death every day. Poverty bred crime, disease, and prostitution in the capital. Public hangings for minor offenses became common, and prisons were packed to overflowing.

In 1816 French aristocrat and fellow Quaker Stephen Grellet persuaded Elizabeth to extend her ministry to women and children incarcerated in London's infamous Newgate Prison. On her first visit she was horrified to find three hundred women and girls confined to two rooms. Some were sentenced to death for minor offenses; others were incarcerated but untried. Many children were the sons and daughters of the inmates; some had been born behind bars. Conditions were so wretched that Elizabeth witnessed prisoners fighting over the clothes of a dead baby.

At that time, Great Britain warehoused 107,000 prisoners, more than all of Europe combined. Overwhelmed by the squalor she observed, Elizabeth retreated to the countryside to carry on her ministry there. She returned three years later, however, determined to improve the prisoners' lot. First she persuaded Newgate's governor to allow her to organize the women inmates into work groups and then she began educating their children.

Elizabeth astonished the prisoners by empowering them to create their own spaces and work groups. An experimental group of seventy women created six rooms at Newgate, including one for sewing and needlework the prisoners could sell, and another as a classroom for thirty children. Quaker textile merchants provided remnants for prisoners to make clothing, and Elizabeth added to each prisoner's work income, so each would have a small nest egg when released. Otherwise prisoners made up their own rules.

Within a year, Newgate's governor noted that his female prisoners were clean, demure, and disciplined. They no longer cursed, gambled, or prostituted themselves to guards for food, because they were employed, empowered, and protected. At Elizabeth's urging, a female matron was hired to protect inmates from the male guards. Although chastised by fellow Quakers for her absences from her children, Elizabeth persisted in her ministry, and her innovations would become the basis for prison reform throughout Europe.

Although she increasingly attracted support from politicians and the wealthy, Elizabeth did experience personal setbacks. During the economic downturn of 1828, for example, the Fry family was forced to declare bankruptcy, and was suspended from its Quaker meeting. Elizabeth's husband and children became embittered, but Elizabeth remained a steadfast Friend. At the same time, she developed a chronic cough and began spitting up blood. Until her death in 1845 her health steadily declined, but her work continued.

Among her innovations were the first "half-way houses," to help transition discharged prisoners back to responsible lives, and detention homes for preadolescent children caught stealing. Instead of being imprisoned, delinquents were closely supervised, attended school, achieved literacy, learned trades, and received religious instruction. In place of flogging and solitary confinement for difficult women prisoners, Elizabeth proposed cutting their hair short. She also was successful in curtailing the use of leg and wrist irons on female prisoners being shipped to Australia.

Through the years, Elizabeth pleaded for rehabilitation rather than increased punishment in her nation's prisons. But by 1836 the government had prevailed in its intention to make prison life a deterrent to crime. In that process, "amateurs" like Elizabeth were replaced by paid officials whose only interest was security. A national police force was created in an attempt to confront crime at its source, and religious instruction was no longer permitted behind bars.

But just as it appeared that Elizabeth had failed in her efforts to reform the treatment of prisoners in her own country, other nations adopted her ideas. Heads of state and tumultuous crowds welcomed Elizabeth and her compassionate innovations in cities throughout France, Holland, Prussia, and Belgium. The treatment of both male and female prisoners on the Continent improved, based on her Newgate model.

Meanwhile, despite her failing health, Elizabeth continued to plead for prison reform not only in her native England, but in Scotland and Ireland as well. On one of her trips to the Continent, she inspired the founding of a teaching hospital in Dusseldorf. It was there that the young Florence Nightingale would learn nursing and launch her own career in the following of Christ.

Exhausted and frail, Elizabeth died in 1845 of a stroke and was buried in the Friends' cemetery in Barking, England. Over a thousand admirers attended her funeral. In both her successes and her failures, Elizabeth did what she believed Jesus would do.

3. Albert Schweitzer

In 1965 the news of Albert Schweitzer's death was first transmitted not by radio, television, or satellite, but by the jungle drums of Gabon in central Africa. Half a century earlier the drums had announced "Oganda, the White Fetishman, has come among us." Now, at the end, they sounded the lament: "Papa Pour Nous is dead."

A week earlier, at his jungle hospital in Africa, Dr. Schweitzer read from the Bible and played an after-supper hymn for the last time. Active to the end, he died on September 4, 1965, at the age of ninety. Thirteen years earlier, Schweitzer had been awarded the Nobel Peace Prize for his efforts on behalf of the "brotherhood of nations," but on his deathbed, he lamented that universal brotherhood remained elusive.

Schweitzer was arguably the last true Renaissance man of the twentieth century: philosopher, theologian, physician, musicologist, author, and world-class organist. Yet, all of his accomplishments could be compressed into one theme: reverence for life. Had he lived longer, Schweitzer surely would have joined forces with environmentalists to save the planet. But Schweitzer considered *all* species on earth to be endangered—not least, humankind itself. He became a healer and peacemaker because he believed humanity was threatened with extinction by mutual destruction. He was moved by the tragedy of two world wars in his lifetime and the prospect of a nuclear holocaust.

Schweitzer was equipped for any number of careers, and would have achieved world-class celebrity in any of them. Instead, at the age of thirty-eight, he became a physician with the sole intention of serving those who suffered for lack of medical care. His wife, Helene, studied nursing so she could assist him.

With the help of natives, the couple built a simple hospital at Lambaréné on the banks of the Ogowe River in what was then French equatorial Africa. The missionary doctor personally financed his work with income from his books and recitals, later supplemented by support from admirers around the world.

No sooner had the physician arrived in Africa during World War I than he was interned by the colonial French government as a German alien. When he sought to return briefly to Europe, he was held in France as a prisoner of war. The irony of being considered an enemy was compounded by the fact that Schweitzer had been born in Alsace, a border province claimed by both France and Germany.

During World War II Schweitzer was literally caught in the crossfire between Vichy French troops occupying Lambaréné and Free French forces on the Gabon mainland. Free French planes routinely strafed the island but spared the hospital. In November 1942, while the doctor was gathering vegetables in the hospital garden, a Vichy machine gunner mistook him for the enemy and sprayed him with bullets. Furious, Schweitzer had a leper patient deliver a note to the Vichy commandant that read:

> Your machine gun nearly killed me this morning. This is a violation of our agreement and of the Geneva Convention which neutralizes hospitals and medical personnel. If you shoot at me again I will prohibit your men from visiting the hospital.

The Vichy commander was so overcome with remorse that he fell ill that night and had to be cared for by the doctor for two weeks.

Albert Schweitzer was not a sentimental humanitarian but a mission doctor determined to bring the gospel to Africa through healing. The eldest son of a Lutheran pastor, he cast his own life in Jesus' footsteps, proposing to become a minister himself in Strasbourg. In 1906 his book, *The Quest of the Historical Jesus*, arguing for the authenticity of Jesus as portrayed in the Gospels, established him as a world figure in theology. In his autobiography, he noted,

> As a young man, my main ambition was to be a good minister . . . I completed my studies; then, after a while I started to teach. I became the principal of the seminary. All this while I had been studying and thinking about the life of Jesus and the meaning of Jesus. And the more I studied and thought, the more convinced I became that Christian theology had become overcomplicated. In the early centuries after Christ, the beautiful simplicities relating to Jesus became . . . obscured.

Simultaneous with his success in theology, Schweitzer became a world-renowned organist. Charles-Marie Widor, his teacher in Paris, rated him the foremost interpreter of

Johann Sebastian Bach, and asked him to make a study of the composer's life and art. When that work was published in 1905, it was touted as the definitive Bach biography. Throughout his life Schweitzer continued to give organ recitals throughout Europe to support his medical and teaching mission in Lambaréné. Because the jungle heat and humidity was inhospitable to musical instruments, he had only a zinc-lined upright piano in his home.

As a young boy, Schweitzer was sensitive to cruelty to animals. One day during Lent, a friend invited him to shoot birds with slingshots. But just as the birds appeared, a church bell rang, which young Albert took as a divine warning. After startling the birds so they would fly from danger, he then ran home. Years later, he confessed that

> . . . ever since, when the Passiontide bells ring out . . .
> I reflect with a rush of grateful emotion how on that
> day their music drove deep into my heart the com-
> mandment: "Thou shalt not kill." This early influ-
> ence upon me of the commandment not to kill or
> torture other creatures is the great experience of my
> childhood and youth.

In 1923, Schweitzer published his *Philosophy of Civiliza-tion*, proposing reverence for life as essential for the survival of civilization. A year later, he returned to Africa to rebuild the hospital, later adding a leper colony. By the time of his death in 1965, there were 350 patients with their relatives at the Schweitzer hospital, and another 150 patients in the colony, served by 36 physicians and nurses, plus native aides. Just as Mother Teresa would attract young volunteers from around the world to her hospital in Calcutta, earlier generations went to Lambaréné to teach, build, cook, clean, and assist the medical staff.

Dr. Schweitzer confined his mission to the jungle, but his example prompted the creation of Doctors Without Borders, mobile healers who now go anywhere in the world where violence threatens the lives of innocent people. They, too, were awarded the Nobel Peace Prize.

At the internment of "Papa Pour Nous," thousands of natives gathered to express their grief and gratitude in song and dance. Many had been cured by the doctor; many others had been born in his hospital. All had found faith through his imitation of Christ.

4. Dorothy Day

Harvard psychiatrist Robert Coles was a medical student in New York City when he first encountered Dorothy Day in 1952 at a soup kitchen on the Lower East Side:

> She was sitting at a table, talking with a woman who was, I quickly realized, quite drunk, yet determined to carry on a conversation . . . When would it end—the alcoholic ranting and the silent nodding, occasionally interrupted by a brief question, which only served, maddeningly, to wind up the already over-talkative one rather than wind her down? Finally, silence fell upon the room. Dorothy Day asked the woman if she would mind an interruption. She got up and came over to me. She said, "Are you waiting to talk with one of us?"

One of us. Her question spoke volumes about how Dorothy Day identified herself with those in need. Could she conceive of Coles being interested in talking with a raving alcoholic? Yes, because Dorothy was interested. No respecter of persons, she honored everyone, convinced that God cares equally and infinitely for all men and women whatever their character or condition. She also knew that many needed more *human* care than others, so she devoted a long life to serving the destitute, the despised, the lonely, the addicted, the homeless, and the afflicted. She embraced their poverty by living among them.

My own introduction to Dorothy Day came about a year after Dr. Coles's encounter with her. She was then in her late fifties. I had been assigned as her student host at Knox College in Galesburg, Illinois, where she had been invited to lecture in the chapel. Speaking of the plight of the poor in personal rather than political terms, her quiet message was that every human being is responsible for every other. She urged the students to dismantle the barriers their forebears had erected between the races and the sexes, the rich and the poor.

In that complacent decade, Day's appeal did not resonate with youth. Later, however, in the '60s, she would march across Mississippi, Louisiana, and Alabama with a more-committed generation, putting her life on the line for civil rights. She was a lifelong fighter for justice, but she was never shrill, never righteously indignant. Rather, she was the calmest rebel imaginable.

But a rebel she was. Born in New York in 1897, Dorothy was raised in Chicago in a family of journalists. At the age of sixteen, she entered the University of Illinois. An indifferent student, she stayed only two years—long enough to develop a passionate sense of injustice in American society. At nineteen she was working in New York as a reporter for the *Call*, a socialist newspaper, writing about the poverty and suffering that accompanied the "return to normalcy" following the First World War. At the age of twenty, Dorothy was jailed in Washington, D.C., for marching with women seeking the right to vote.

For the next few years, Day drifted, idealistic but without religious faith, in the company of radical writers and bohemians, among them Max Eastman, John Dos Passos, and Eugene O'Neill. She became pregnant during an unhappy love affair with a tough ex-journalist, had an abortion, and married another unsuitable man on the rebound. She took to drinking heavily, and they separated permanently after only a year. Her ex-husband would go on to have eight wives.

Returning to Chicago, Dorothy was jailed briefly for demonstrating for workers' rights. Her experience behind bars, confined in the company of prostitutes and society's castoffs, haunted her for the remainder of her life. She spoke fondly of one streetwalker in her cell who had befriended her:

> I can still hear Mary-Ann giving me my lessons in survival—how to get along with the people running the prison. "You must hold up your head high, and give them no clue that you're afraid of them or

ready to beg them for anything, any favors whatsoever. But you must see them for what they are—
never forget that they're in jail, too." Many times, so
many times, I remember that admonition. Mary-
Ann had no use for organized religion . . . but in her
head and her heart she had somehow drawn near
our Lord. Nearer than I was able to get, then. Who
knows, nearer than some of us ever get.

Dorothy began reading the Bible while in prison. While
she continued to work at odd jobs and pose for art classes
to eke out a living, her family accused her of slumming.
That, however, was hardly her purpose; rather, Day was
attempting to learn firsthand what people were forced to
do to earn a living. Making friends with muckraking journalists Ben Hecht and Charles MacArthur, she investigated
how harshly courts treated juveniles and prostitutes. In
New Orleans she wrote sympathetically about the insecure
lives of dance-hall girls. During these years she wrote a
semi-autobiographical novel, *The Eleventh Virgin*, which
was bought by Hollywood.

In 1925, on Staten Island, Day entered a common-law
marriage with Forster Batterham, a biologist by profession
and anarchist and atheist by persuasion. A daughter, Tamar
Teresa, was born to the couple eight months before
Dorothy's thirtieth birthday. To celebrate, Dorothy had her
child baptized in the Catholic Church—and then
announced that she would also be baptized. It was a conversion Forster could not accept, so Dorothy moved with
her infant daughter to an apartment in lower Manhattan to
be close to Our Lady of Guadalupe Church.

Day became a fervent convert but didn't know how to
turn her new faith into a dedicated life. For a time she
worked for the Fellowship for Reconciliation, then went to
Hollywood as a screenwriter, but found life in California to
be artificial. By this time, the Great Depression had set in,
and Dorothy witnessed more poverty than ever before. She
felt that Christ's example and admonitions were being
ignored not only by government and society, but by the
Church itself. Rather than criticize the Church, however,
she prayed for it.

In her autobiography *The Long Loneliness,* Day cites Pope Pius XI as saying that "the workers of the world are lost to the Church"—Dorothy would dedicate the rest of her life to proving the pope wrong. To facilitate her following of Christ, she took personal vows of poverty, chastity, and obedience. The young divorced mother determined to "die in order to live," and shunned romantic involvement altogether.

In Washington just before Christmas 1932, Day witnessed what she called a small army of desperately impoverished people who were pleading for food, for a chance to work, and to assert their dignity as citizens. Dorothy prayed for the opportunity to use her talents on their behalf. Then, on her return to New York, she was introduced to a French pacifist, Peter Maurin, a layman who had taken similar vows. For the remainder of their lives, these two pilgrims became spiritual siblings and close collaborators, reminiscent of St. Clare and St. Francis of Assisi many centuries earlier. Together they created the *Catholic Worker* movement and produced an eight-page monthly newspaper, the Catholic Worker, which would forever sell for just a penny a copy to make it affordable to the poor. Within a few years it had a circulation of 150,000.

Together, Dorothy and Peter rented a storefront and an apartment where they could feed, clothe, and house the homeless, live with them and offer them friendship and affection. In time, like-minded people gathered to help the two, and soon were more than thirty "houses of hospitality" in cities across the nation, plus farms that offered both refuge and employment to the destitute. Local *Catholic Worker* movement newspapers sprang up in American cities as well as in England and Australia.

From May Day 1933 until November 29, 1980, when she died at the age of eighty, Dorothy Day kept and lived her vows. Tamar, her daughter, married and made Dorothy a grandmother many times over. Just before her death, she told Robert Coles:

> I try to remember this life that the Lord gave me; the other day I wrote down the words "a life remembered," and I was going to make a summary for

myself, write what mattered most—but I couldn't do it. I just sat there and thought of our Lord, and his visit to us all those centuries ago, and I said to myself that my great luck was to have had him on my mind for so long in my life.

✎ ✎ ✎

These are four very different disciples, each of whom chose a different path to follow Christ. Not one of them was conventionally pious; on the contrary, all were irreverent and outspoken in their own way. While not self-righteous, they were—most of the time—right. These were cranky saints: Schweitzer and Snyder inclined to arrogance, Fry to vanity and celebrity, Day to carelessness in her youth. But all had this in common: they did not let their flaws interfere with their dedication. All, in their own time and to their own capacity, did what Jesus would have done. Like him, they left the world a better place for their presence in it.

It is tempting to become discouraged when confronted with the example of such single-minded people. But we need not be heroic or saintly in order to follow Jesus—just humble and consistent and determined.

Until recently, the U.S. Army attracted recruits to serve our country with the promise: "Be all that you can be." Now its appeal to each recruit is to become "an Army of one." To be all that we can be we must follow Christ in *our* way, not someone else's. Edward Everett Hale, who wrote *The Man Without a Country*, spoke as a disciple when he affirmed:

> I am only one,
> But still I am one.
> I cannot do everything,
> But still I can do something;
> And because I cannot do everything
> I will not refuse to do the something I can.

Questions to Ponder

1. What problem can you solve by imitating Christ? Which problems will remain?
2. What kinship to you feel with Snyder, Fry, Schweitzer, and Day?
3. What motivated each of the profiled persons in this chapter to imitate Christ? What is your motive for imitating Christ?
4. Did it matter that, although dedicated, all the persons profiled in this chapter remained flawed? Explain.
5. What did Jesus mean when he told his disciples to be "wise as serpents and harmless as doves?"

Following in Jesus' Steps

1. *Mitch Snyder.* Was the good he accomplished outweighed by his early abandonment of his family and his final self-destruction? Can I do good despite my handicap?
2. *Elizabeth Fry.* In the United States today, two million men and women are imprisoned, and little or no attention is paid to their rehabilitation. Does this mean Elizabeth Fry's mission was a failure? Explain. How can I act to reconcile others?
3. *Albert Schweitzer.* Dr. Schweitzer confined himself to healing and teaching natives in an obscure jungle hospital in Africa. What lessons did his mission provide to Christians elsewhere in the world? How can I be a healer?
4. *Dorothy Day.* Was Dorothy Day helped or hindered by her Church? What assistance can I draw from the Church in imitating Christ?

The Big Question

How can I best devote my particular talents to the service of Christ and humankind?

EIGHT

THE MIND
OF THE DISCIPLE

Johann Sebastian Bach dedicated every piece of music he ever composed, both religious and secular, "to the greater glory of God." God, of course, doesn't require greater glory than he already possesses; he is beyond flattery. But Bach, like other Christians who dedicate their lives to their Creator, was impelled by gratitude. He, indeed, was a disciple.

God is the only true philanthropist; the best we can do is to be thankful for our very existence and every subsequent blessing. G. K. Chesterton, raised without religion, found his way to faith in God as an adult because he needed someone to be grateful *to*. Every disciple of Jesus, motivated by gratitude, expresses that gratitude in loving service.

The ultimate answer to "What are we to do?" was provided by St. Augustine when Christianity was still young. At first glance, his counsel—to "love God and do what you will"—might appear to be moral license. Yet, it is anything but! The Christian who loves God wills what God wills. "Thy will be done on earth" is the essence of the Lord's Prayer and the controlling motive of those who would imitate Christ.

Human beings are the only moral creatures in the universe, because we alone enjoy a freedom of action that God withheld from the rest of his creation. But every situation we meet in our lives is not a moral dilemma. For example,

I set my alarm for seven each morning by habit. I eat, sleep, work, relax, and exercise of necessity—none of which involves moral decision making. Christians know in some detail what God and society expect of us. It is only on those occasions when we are unsure whether we owe more to God, to ourselves, and to others that we are prompted to ask "What are we to do?"

THE TRUE DISCIPLE

Many people avoid this critical question altogether by eluding the occasions in which it must be asked. They insulate themselves and do little or nothing to meet the needs of others. By contrast, disciples of Jesus welcome situations that make demands on them—as Jesus said:

> "I was hungry and you gave me food. I was thirsty and you gave me a drink. I was lonely and you made me welcome. I was naked and you clothed me. I was ill and you came and looked after me. I was in prison and you came to see me there."
>
> Puzzled, his disciples asked:
>
> "Lord, when did we see you hungry and give you food? When did we see you thirsty and give you something to drink? When did we see you lonely and make you welcome, or see you naked and clothe you, or see you ill or in prison and go to see you?"
>
> Jesus assured them that "whatever you did for the humblest of my brothers you did for me" (Matthew 25:34–40).

The piety of a true disciple is not posture but service. To ask "What are we to do?" is a constant exercise in humility, not righteousness. By contrast, cocksure Christians ape the Pharisees, whom Jesus castigated as "miserable frauds" (Matthew 23:25), "serpents" (23:33), "blind leaders" (23:16), and "play actors" (23:15)—"for you appear like good men on the outside, but inside you are a mass of pretense" (23:28). They seldom ask, "What are we to do?" assuming they already know.

As true disciples of Jesus, we avoid forcing our faith on others as if we possess utter certainty. Faith is a gift that is God's to award, not ours to insist on, and of necessity it lives alongside doubt. We share our faith not by argument and appeals to human frailty, but by good example and appeals to the best in others—thus drawing others to faith because they see that it has made a disciple a better person. That is the good news we share through service.

IMITATING JESUS

The following of Christ, of necessity, is only approximate. After all, Jesus lived in a place, time, and context distinct from our own, and was impelled by a mission unique to himself—the redemption of humankind.

Only a lunatic could pretend to *be* Jesus. For the rest of us it is possible to be Christ-*like*; indeed, it is imperative to imitate him because he set the standard for what God had in mind when he created moral creatures with the capacity to love. The following of Christ, however, demands more than courtesy and good manners. As Jesus made clear, we must do as he did—"give up all right to himself, and take up his cross" (Matthew 16:24).

This is where true disciples must draw on true faith. After all, aren't there enough crosses to bear in life without carrying Jesus' as well? Life is already fraught with tragedies—illness, accident, loss, physical and mental decline, violence, unrequited love, and impoverishment among them. Why make it harder on ourselves?

Because Jesus did, and he did it for us. That, in turn, makes following Christ an act of gratitude. Even more: it becomes a vindication of God's gift of life and Jesus' gift of his own life. The ultimate gift still awaits us: God's kingdom.

But how do we follow Christ in the twenty-first century? We begin with the Beatitudes, converting our hearts and minds to be humble, sorrowful, undemanding, hungry and thirsty for justice, merciful, sincere, peacemaking, grateful, and forgiving. These are the signs of discipleship in every age and place, the standards in God's kingdom.

Given all we understand about living the Sermon on the Mount, we next ask "Is it possible to become such a person?" Jesus answered: "Humanly speaking it is impossible; but with God anything is possible" (Matthew 19:26).

How Jesus Acted

The Beatitudes define the character of the disciple, but they fall short of answering the question "What are we to do?" Even after this careful exploration of the Sermon on the Mount, we can call to mind the many situations today that leave us perplexed, even as disciples of Jesus, and the question remains pressing. There really is no better way to answer it than to look directly at how Jesus consistently acted, how he responded to the details of life in his own time.

Jesus dealt with people directly. Jesus was not an organization man. Rather, he paid attention to the details. He confronted men and women, friends and foes alike, face to face, personally. Although he preached to the masses, he called, cured, and counseled people individually. His apostles were not recruited *en masse* but one-by-one, each one personally called. Jesus laid hands on the sick, forgave sins, and restored life by personal involvement.

Today, many disciples are inclined to avoid direct contact. We prefer, rather, to address people's needs through charitable agencies, leaving it to social workers, health professionals, and bureaucrats to deal with the actual individuals. It is possible (and even likely) to commit oneself to alleviating homelessness, hunger, and drug abuse, or finding a cure for cancer without ever meeting a homeless, hungry, addicted man or woman, or cancer victim.

Doubtless, organizations are more effective over the long term than individual caregivers, but those needing assistance require more than vouchers, welfare checks, and food stamps. They need the personal concern of individuals who know their names and sense their plight.

Christians who take discipleship seriously become involved in their churches; and that is a good thing. Unfortunately, one can exhaust oneself in church work to the exclusion of personal service. Jesus did not sing in a church choir or raise funds for church construction. His priorities were not institutional but personal. He delivered the Good News directly and individually.

Jesus was not a loner. From the outset Jesus depended on others, relying on his parents, submitting to baptism by John, then calling his apostles, gathering disciples, and encouraging the faith communities of the early church. Although he was clearly their leader, he enrolled and empowered others to preach the gospel, to forgive, and to cure. When he sent his disciples on missions of their own, he sent them not alone but in pairs. Christians ever since have formed communities and worked, prayed, and served together.

In the chaos that followed the collapse of Rome beginning in the late fourth century, many Christians fled the empire's cities to become hermits, celebrated for their eccentric and exaggerated piety. In time, the monastic movement gathered these zealots into economically self-sufficient brotherhoods and sisterhoods, where they were tested by living and serving in the spirit of Christian love. Disciples in our own time cannot confine their spiritual lives to reading, religious television, or chat rooms on the Internet. Rather, they must join with others in prayer and mutual service.

Jesus hated sin but loved sinners. Jesus was quick to forgive, even before sinners acknowledged repentance. Typically, he combined forgiveness of sin with the cure of physical maladies—underscoring the fact that forgiveness is itself a cure. His sole requirement was that sinners seek to reform their lives. With Jesus, it was never too late to be forgiven. Even from his cross of death he forgave the thief suffering alongside him. Had Judas the traitor sought forgiveness rather than succumbing to despair, Jesus would have offered it. In the final moments of his life, Jesus forgave his torturers and executioners—not because they showed remorse but because they were ignorant of their injustice.

Anyone who asks "What are we to do?" must acknowledge that, like Jesus, we are to be quick to forgive friends, enemies, and strangers alike. Moreover, we are to prefer the company of sinners. How else could Jesus forgive transgressors if he did not know them well enough to confront them with their shortcomings? The same is true for us.

Jesus clearly distinguished between sins of the weak and sins of the powerful. He was gentle with the woman taken in adultery and harsh with the hypocritical Pharisees who condemned her. "Let the one among you who has never sinned throw the first stone," he warned. After her accusers dispersed in shame, Jesus demanded, "Where are they all—did no one condemn you? . . . Neither do I condemn you . . . Go away now and do not sin again" (John 8:7–9).

To be sure, much of life's unpleasantness is caused by something less than sin. People irritate and bore one another; they become impatient, vulgar, and unlikeable. Customer service representatives can keep us on hold on the telephone interminably. Indeed, these are human frailties that do not require God's forgiveness, but demand ours.

To forgive is to unburden oneself, whether or not another's sin is acknowledged by its perpetrator. Today, among Christians, there are honest differences of opinion as to what constitutes sin—be it war, abortion, homosexuality, euthanasia, or the like. In the confusion of uncertainty, what are we to do? We follow Jesus; we forgive. Like Jesus, we hate the sin and love the sinner.

Jesus regarded life as a blessing, not a predicament. Thomas Hobbes, in *Leviathan*, warning against a soaring birth rate, predicted that overpopulation would render human life "nasty, brutish, and short." The English philosopher was but one in a long line of pessimists that extends to this day.

Jesus, by contrast, celebrated life. He counted its blessings and was grateful for his Father's providence that sustains the lilies of the field and birds of the air. "Never be afraid," he told his disciples, "you are far more valuable than sparrows" (Matthew 10:31).

Whoever treats life as a predicament rather than a blessing fails to appreciate that the Son of God hallowed life by becoming human, extending hope to every person no matter how needy. Unfortunately, there is a perverse streak in human nature that dramatizes life's difficulties, preferring problems to solutions. Human drama thrives on conflict. We are made to feel important as stars of our own small tragedies. But that was not Jesus' way. In his humility, Jesus looked past conflict to bring about resolution.

It is not an exaggeration to say that Jesus viewed life as comedy (albeit a divine one) rather than as tragedy. Comedies are plots about characters who act foolishly, but they have happy endings. Tragedies, on the other hand, have players who are betrayed by their flaws, and they end badly. Jesus amply convinced his disciples of their own shortsightedness and foolishness, and he assured them of the happiest of endings.

The story of Jesus is not a tragedy, because he had no tragic flaw to account for his premature death on the cross. His death was due to human folly; by dying he ensured a happy ending for humankind. Accordingly, his disciples in any age must be lighthearted and hopeful—not cockeyed optimists, of course, but self-assured. Only then will they be able to devote their lives to others rather than worrying about themselves. In the prologue to his Gospel, St. John celebrates Jesus for bringing light to life:

> In him appeared life and this life was the light of mankind. The light still shines in the darkness and the darkness has never put it out . . . So the word of God became a human being and lived among us. We saw his glory (the glory like that of a father's only son), full of grace and truth (John 1:4–5; 14).

Jesus' example to those who would follow him is to celebrate life, as he did, and to live in certain hope. Jesus was joyful.

Jesus prayed. The Rev. Eugene Rivers leads the Pentecostal Azuza Christian Community in a crime-ridden, impoverished section of Boston that police call Beirut West. When Rev. Rivers recruits recent black graduates of Harvard and MIT to return to the neighborhood to redeem it, he warns them, "If you don't pray, don't come!"

The point of prayer is that nothing good gets done without God's collaboration. Considering that he was God's Son, we might assume that Jesus' prayers were just friendly, intimate conversations with his Father. In fact, they were poignant pleadings, not unlike our own. Obviously, the only prayers of Jesus contained in the New Testament are those overheard by his disciples, but they are sufficient to characterize the nature of his pleas.

We have already considered the Lord's Prayer—the one Jesus offered as a model in the course of his Sermon on the Mount. It is a complete prayer, praising God, affirming his will, expressing hope and repentance, seeking and promising forgiveness, and asking for the necessities of life. But Scripture offers numerous other insights into the prayer life of Jesus.

Shortly before he died in the first year of the new millennium, former archbishop of Canterbury Donald Coggan presented me with his book, *The Prayers of the New Testament*. Here is a sample of how Jesus prayed and what he prayed for:

> "O Father, Lord of Heaven and earth, I thank you for hiding these things from the clever and intelligent and for showing them to mere children" (Matthew 11:25).

> "Father, I thank you that you have heard me. I know that you always hear me, but I have said this for the sake of these people standing here so that they may believe that you have sent me" (John 11:42).

> "Now comes my hour of heart-break, and what can I say, "Father, save me from this hour"? No, it was for this very purpose that I came to this hour. Father, honor your own name!" (John 12:27–28)

> "My Father, if it is possible let this cup pass from me—yet it must not be what I want, but what you want . . . My Father, if it is not possible for this cup to pass from me without my drinking it, then your will must be done" (Matthew 26:39; 42).

"Father, forgive them; they do not know what they are doing" (Luke 23:34).

"Father, I commend my spirit into your hands" (Luke 23:46).

In his longest prayer, Jesus prayed to his Father for his disciples. Here are excerpts:

> "This is eternal life, to know you, the only true God, and him whom you have sent Jesus Christ . . . I have shown your self to the men whom you gave me from the world. They were your men and you gave them to me, and they have accepted your word . . . I am praying to you for them . . . for they are yours . . . Holy Father, keep the men you gave me by the power that they may be one, as we are one . . . I have given them your word, and the world has hated them, for they are no more sons of the world than I am—make them Holy by the truth . . . Father, I want those whom you have given me to be with me where I am. I want them to see that glory which you have made mine—for you loved me before the world began" (John 17).

Jesus lived simply. We misunderstand simplicity if we think of it as self-denial. Rather, simplicity unburdens us, allowing us to focus not on the things we own which we fear losing but on the real treasures of life. What we do not have cannot be taken from us. Simplicity enriches the disciple.

Thomas Merton was distraught when, in the winter of 1965, a refrigerator was delivered to his Kentucky hermitage. The most renowned exponent of the simple life in the twentieth century had spent years persuading his Trappist superiors to permit him to live alone on the monastery grounds. How, he asked himself, could he justify such a big, modern appliance sharing his solitude?

Merton's discomfiture prompted one of the monk's lasting insights—that true simplicity is *internal*, not to be measured by a paucity of possessions but by singleness of spirit. Although simple living is practical, convenient, and economical, it becomes spiritual only when it is internalized.

Few of us are prepared to follow literally Jesus' counsel to the rich young man in the Gospels: to sell all he had, give the proceeds to the poor, then join the master. Today's disciples, however, can convert external simplicity into internal spirituality. Happily, unless we resist the spiritual transformation, it will happen of its own accord.

There is a serendipity to this simplifying process. As we simplify our circumstances we develop greater awareness, sensitivity, and singleness of purpose. With less to distract us, we open ourselves to a fresh sense of wonder and appreciation of simple gifts. Our minds become uncluttered and our faith stronger and simpler. We find the time and the inclination to get outside of ourselves and serve others, as Jesus did.

America's great philosopher of simplicity, Henry David Thoreau, remarked in *Walden* that "insofar as one simplifies his life, the laws of the universe will appear less complex, and solitude will not be solitude, nor poverty poverty, nor weakness weakness."

"Love your life," Thoreau urged. "Meet it and live it; do not shun it and call it hard names. . . . Only that day dawns to which we are awake. There is more day to dawn. The sun is but a morning star."

Jesus spoke the truth. When Jesus concluded his Sermon on the Mount, "the crowd were astonished at the power behind his teaching. For his words had the ring of authority . . ." (Matthew 7:28–29).

One of the sadder developments of recent times is that tolerance is valued more than truth. Jesus, however, knew better: some things are, in fact, intolerable. It is why he lashed out at the Pharisees and overturned the money changers' tables in the Temple. It is why he called the apostle Peter "Satan" for tempting him to abandon his mission. Because criminal behavior is intolerable, two million Americans are currently behind bars.

For years I have been privileged to write a syndicated newspaper column about topics that concern people of faith. More often than I wish, something I have written offends a reader and I hear about it. Usually the problem is that I have challenged a prejudice that a reader has incorporated into his or her religious faith.

The reason faith is not a topic for discussion in polite company is that many people, Christians among them, consider faith to be strictly personal. They are wrong; faith is either true or false. Jesus punctured people's presumptions when he preached the Good News of the gospel in his own time and place. The fact that Christianity in the United States today is represented by a thousand distinct denominations reflects conflicting interpretations of what the gospel demands of us. But it does not relieve us of the responsibility of spreading that gospel, let alone jettisoning our common faith.

Jesus was not arrogant in his preaching. He did not seek to crush his opponents, but to give them the gift of Good News. That he escaped his persecutors' death judgment as long as he did testifies to the way he told the truth. Instead of barking commandments, he wrapped the truth in parables that carried a moral. And when his critics sought to trap him with questions, he turned their challenges back, defusing them:

> "Let the one among who has never sinned throw the first stone" (John 8:7).

> "Then give the Caesar the things that belong to Caesar, and to God the things that belong to God" (Matthew 22:21).

> "The Sabbath was made for man's sake; man was not made for the sake of the Sabbath" (Mark 2:27).

Jesus managed to be authoritative without being argumentative. It is a good lesson for his disciples, who will impress more by example than contentiousness.

SO . . . WHAT ARE WE TO DO?

Even a cursory reading of the Gospels reveals how Jesus dealt with life and people. The answer to "What are we to do?" in our situation will become apparent when we do what the saints did: put on the mind of Christ, aligning our wills with his. In our efforts to do so, we know a lot. We know, for example, how Jesus

- treated parents, friends, enemies, officials, women, children, strangers, the rich, the poor, and sinners
- acted when confronted by treachery
- handled emotion
- spoke out and when he kept his peace
- celebrated, what he celebrated, and when he abstained
- prayed and what he prayed for
- valued others and what he despised
- regarded violence
- thought and what he considered worth a miracle
- loved

Because Jesus refused to regard life as a tragedy, we can agree with G. K. Chesterton that joy is the gigantic secret of the Christian. Chesterton said of Jesus:

> His pathos was natural, almost casual. The Stoics, ancient and modern, were proud of concealing their tears. He never concealed his tears; he showed them plainly on his open face at any daily sight, such as the far sight of his native city. Yet he concealed something. Solemn supermen and imperial diplomatists are proud of restraining their anger. He never restrained his anger. He flung furniture down the front steps of the Temple, and asked men how they expected to escape the damnation of hell. Yet he restrained something. I say it with reverence; there was in that shattering personality a thread that must be called shyness. There was something that he hid from all men when he went up a mountain to pray. There was something that he covered

constantly by abrupt silence or impetuous isolation. There was some one thing that was too great for God to show us when he walked upon our earth; and I have sometimes fancied that it was his mirth.

A Disciple's Prayer

My favorite prayer is one I borrowed years ago from the late headmaster of St. Alban's School, Washington, D.C. In life, the Rev. Charles Martin and his dog were inseparable. So Canon Martin asked God:

> Lord, help me to be the person
> my dog thinks me to be.

In its own way, Martin's prayer expresses what we all seek by living the Sermon on the Mount. If you have a dog, as I do, you are the constant object of its devotion, trust, and gratitude. For the smallest of personal investment, a dog will be faithful to you for life. Dogs have been known to save their masters from death, and have even died for them. A dog's delight in its master's very presence is poignant, because it is so utterly undeserved. My own Scottish terrier not only greets me by wagging her tail but by running in circles.

No man or woman merits such devotion, any more than we deserve Jesus' sacrifice of himself for us. But we can do and be better. With grace and effort we can become the persons God had in mind when he created us and gave his Son to die for us. We can live the Sermon on the Mount. Jesus promised as much: "Humanly speaking it is impossible," he said, "but with God anything is possible."

Questions to Ponder

1. What does Augustine mean when he counsels, "Love God and do what you will"?

2. How do we express our gratitude to God for our lives and to Jesus for our redemption?

3. When does human behavior become moral or immoral?

4. What are the best ways of sharing our religious faith?

5. Are we following Jesus when we devote ourselves to good causes? Explain.

Following in Jesus' Steps

1. *Discipleship.* What do I understand Jesus to mean when he says, "If anyone wants to follow in my footsteps, he must give up all right to himself"?

2. *Virtue.* Can I sin without feeling guilty? Can I be good without feeling virtuous?

3. *Service.* Is serving the Church the same as loving God and serving my neighbor?

4. *Forgiveness.* What does it mean to me to hate sin but love the sinner?

5. *Tolerance.* When is my tolerance a virtue? When is it an evasion?

The Big Question

How can I speak the truth through my behavior?

NOTES AND ACKNOWLEDGMENTS

I set about this book at my wife's urging. In later years, after our children had left the nest, we began worshiping as Quakers, drawn to the quiet and peace-loving Society of Friends because of its simplicity. Quakers make do without clergy, sermons, seminaries, liturgy, sacraments, hymns, creeds, churches, employees, and even collection plates. They subsist with the example of Jesus and the promise of his Father, and with the two great commandments: love God and neighbor.

Sitting in utter silence, without distraction, week after week in the company of people who call themselves Friends forces one to discover the God who dwells in each of us, and to turn in love to the needs of others. In such a setting, the Sermon on the Mount is an inescapable subject of meditation and action, and the imitation of Christ is an obvious imperative.

I cannot pretend to have told you anything new about the imitation of Christ in these pages, but only to have freshly considered his Sermon on the Mount, rediscovering its idealism and urgency. We who live by faith need motivation and direction, not novelty.

When G. K. Chesterton wrote *Orthodoxy*, his classic case for Christianity, he subtitled it *The Romance of Faith*. The imitation of Christ is a romantic adventure in faith, because it attempts to emulate the most loving and lovable person who has ever lived.

In these texts, I have used J. B. Phillips's revised translation, not least because it is fresh and unfamiliar. Jesus spoke in Aramaic—not in Greek, Latin, or any modern language. We know what he said but can only approximate *how* he said things. I can imagine Jesus talking this way to us.

⁊ ⁊ ⁊

For reference, I have relied principally on John R. W. Stott's *The Message of the Sermon on the Mount* (InterVarsity Press, 1978), Dale C. Allison's *The Sermon on the Mount* (Crossroad, 1999), and Philip Yancey's *The Jesus I Never Knew* (Zondervan, 1995). My wife brought her dog-eared and underlined student copy of Dietrich Bonhoeffer's *The Cost of Discipleship* (Macmillan, 1963) into our marriage as a kind of dowry. It was invaluable.

I also borrowed from two of my earlier books: *Breaking through God's Silence* (Simon & Schuster, 1996) in chapter three, and from *Be Strong and Courageous* (Sheed & Ward, 2000) in chapter six. The profile of Elizabeth Fry in chapter seven comes from a lecture my wife gave in her series, Celebrated Quaker Women. For the profiles of "Four Who Followed," I relied on George Marshall and David Poling, *Schweitzer, A Biography* (Doubleday, 1971), James Brabazon, *Albert Schweitzer, A Biography* (Putnam, 1975), Albert Schweitzer, *Out of My Life and Thought* (Johns Hopkins, 1998), June Rose, *Elizabeth Fry* (London: Quaker Home Service, 1994), and Robert Coles, *Dorothy Day: A Radical Devotion* (Addison-Wesley, 1987). Alas, biographers have bypassed the late Mitch Snyder, so I relied on newspaper and magazine accounts of his life and work.

⁊ ⁊ ⁊

I was encouraged and assisted by my friends, the late Donald Coggan, 101st archbishop of Canterbury, and by the Rev. John W. Crossin, OSFS, executive director of the Washington Theological Consortium. This book is dedi-